New Book, 1.4

22.95

YOUR ONLY
MUSIC

83

UPROAR'S YOUR ONLY MUSIC

BRIAN BRETT

TORONTO

Ǝ

Exile Editions
2004

This edition is published by Exile Editions Limited, 20 Dale Ave.,
Toronto, Ontario, M4W 1K4 Canada

Sales Distribution:
McArthur & Company c/o Harper Collins
1995 Markham Road, Toronto, ON M1B 5M8
toll free: 1 800 387 0117   (fax) 1 800 668 5788

Composition & Design by MICHAEL CALLAGHAN
Cover Photo by TOM BULLOCK
Typeset at MOONS OF JUPITER, TORONTO, ONTARIO
Printed and Bound at GAUVIN IMPRIMERIE, HULL, QUEBEC

Permission to use the image of the Burning Man granted by BURNING
MAN

Earlier versions and excerpts from the collection have appeared in
The Saanich Review, Mocambo Nights, River King Poetry Supplement,
B.C. Studies, Brick, and There is a Season: A Memoir in a Garden by
Patrick Lane.

The author wishes to thank the Canada Council, The Yukon Libraries
and Archives, and the B.C. Arts Council for their support.

Many thanks to Margaret Atwood. Copy edited by Heidi Greco.

The publisher wishes to acknowledge the
assistance toward publication of the
Canada Council.

ISBN 1-55096-607-3

For
Leonard Francis Brett
June 4, 1920 – May 9, 1998
&
Mary Rose Brett

"All that you can become is yourself."

—*Timothy Findley, in conversation*

Uproar's Your Only Music
A MEMOIR

My grandmother was a flower girl in Piccadilly. Her first husband was shot through the Bible in World War I. The authorities in charge dutifully sent back the Bible saturated with his heart's dark blood. Grandmother, left impoverished with two infants, fell into the arms of her dead husband's brother and soon married him. Another son was born, my father — Leonard — within earshot of Bow Bells, the mark of a true Cockney. When my father was only months old the family emigrated to a better life in the promised land of Canada, bringing the heart-stained Bible which, years later, shocked itself into my consciousness.

In Vancouver, Father's Cockney family was a hard-working bunch: junk collectors and scrap metal dealers, coal deliverymen, door-to-door peddlers of tomatoes, apples, potatoes — anything they could sell. It was a tough house. My father, when still a child, found his father's revolver under a pillow and chased his younger brother Jack through the rooms, laughing and calling out: "I'm going to shoot you!" Then the gun went off.

Jack barely survived. He wore the ugly scar on his spine until he died a decade ago, and my father carried the guilt.

My rollie-smoking granny continued peddling produce into her eighties, until a car erupted out of the rain one night as she was wending her way home after another epic day spent hammering on doors, a potato in one hand and an apple in the other. The car crippled her hip, finished her career, and she turned bitter.

Father grew up on the gritty East End streets and learned how to thrive in that rough-and-tumble world. He used to climb the girders of Vancouver's bridges, shimmying along the rusty steel, sometimes hundreds of feet above the muddy Fraser River, collecting pigeon squabs from their nests. He'd sell the squabs to Chinese gourmands. During my childhood I raised both racing and 'fancy' pigeons, and Father once talked me into taking a box of my extra squabs to China-town. I hadn't put down the box for five minutes before the scuttling baby feet inside attracted a bidding war between a gaggle of old men who appeared out of nowhere. I loved those squabs, though, and felt guilty for years afterwards.

Another day, when I came home, I discovered Father had the squabs from a pair of my best racing pigeons sizzling in the frying pan. I was horrified. Besides, they tasted rubbery.

The pigeons taught me how to love the bird mind, how to appreciate the other unfathomable minds among what we call animals. I've always felt this enormous affinity with animals, especially birds. I can remember standing in the big coop, the pigeons perched on my head, shoulders, and outstretched arms, their gentle cooing, and those bottomless eyes as they shat on me.

The rollers would perform magnificent, looping, controlled flights like World War I aces showing off. The speckled tumblers were most after my own heart. They would climb high into the sky, and then fall, tumbling chaotically until just before they hit the ground, when they would suddenly pull out of the dive and climb back into the sky.

I loved the way the homers circled after a long-distance flight and then plummeted to the landing. One day, Rocky, my adored half-breed homer, perched on a hydro pole before his traditional dash for the trapdoor of the pen — a bad habit common to some pigeons. As he stood there, a diving hawk knocked his head off. Forty years later I can still see that pigeon head shooting into the sky.

Father's parents were famous locally for keeping a one-legged attack rooster named Charlie (his other leg froze off in a cold winter) who was so vicious the mailman wouldn't enter the yard. Charlie used to leap up and rip my mother's stocking when she came for a visit — often drawing blood with his single, clawed foot.

For various now-unknown reasons, I decided I hated my grandparents' home. I'd spend hours waiting outside in our car, stubbornly refusing to go in. I was a hardheaded little kid, blind to the vibrant life inside that rugged household. It was my loss.

With Father's relatives simple events could escalate quickly into scary situations. During a family picnic at Paradise Valley, my cousin Stevie and I started a fight. His dad, Albert, hit me, and my dad hit Albert for hitting me. The whole family joined the fracas and it escalated into a brawl. Afterwards, they found Stevie and me hiding together under the picnic table, and they had to take Father to the hospital to sew back on the piece of ear that Albert had bitten off. Stevie was a beautiful kid who was later decapitated in an elevator shaft at a mine when he was barely nineteen.

My father lost his left leg at the age of seventeen after driving a stolen car into a telephone pole at ninety-seven miles an hour. The accident and a brutal year in hospital knocked some sense into him and he turned away from his shadier East Side friends, though he retained a mischievous heart that would surge up at unexpected moments.

Years later, he told me that when he was released from the hospital he went to work in his Uncle Jim's small mill, on the greenchain — the worst job in the famously brutal lumber industry — hopping on one leg, pulling heavy boards away from the blade and stacking them, until a new, artificial leg could be handmade for him. I witnessed Father's prowess with lumber more than a few times. He'd grasp one end of a long plank, whipping it up and down, using that whipsaw action to flip it onto another pile. Judging from his skill, he worked more than once at the greenchain; then again, the stories he told me could have been just several more in a lifetime of tall tales. Right up until he died he had young children believing his yarns about wrestling the shark, the grizzly bear, or the crocodile that had bitten off his leg.

Father shattered wooden legs at an alarming rate. His best leg was made out of aluminum. It had been willed to him by a deceased customer. That leg lasted for a decade. His record was three destroyed legs in one year. He accidentally felled a tree on the third wooden leg while distracted by a screaming neighbour who was irate because he thought the tree was on his side of the property line — which later, to Father's embarrassment, proved correct. Mother and I accompanied Father to the shop for its replacement. We wanted to see how he'd explain smashing it up so spectacularly.

The health care prosthetics expert couldn't understand this carnage. He said to my father: "These legs are designed by professionals to last a lifetime. This is your third wrecked leg in a year. You are awfully hard on them. What do you do?"

"Well," my father replied, "I ain't no cripple, y'know." The prosthetic expert's eyes widened, and my mother and I leaned against the wall, trying to hold back the laughter. Nothing crippled him, let alone a mere missing leg. When, in his sixties, he was given a sticker allowing him to park in handicapped areas, he was convinced he'd pulled another fast one on the government. Nobody could persuade him that he was handicapped.

Nor did he find his missing limb humiliating, as some people do; though there was an incident when he was carrying a sack of spuds into a lady's house and his foot fell off. The woman let out a little squeak, and then stared at us in horror. It was one of the few times I saw my father lose his cool, as he turned and fled, hopping down the sidewalk. I muttered an explanation to her and hustled after him, hanging onto the woolen sock with his foot and shoe still in it.

He used to keep his broken legs — he'd strip them for parts — hanging on the wall in the basement bathroom, along with a spare he kept for emergencies. This could startle people. On my twelfth birthday I had a party, and one of the kids went looking for the bathroom. The light was off and the legs hanging from the wall sent him screaming down the street.

Throughout his life my father joyfully embraced any job that promised an income. He was only ten years old when the Depression began, and he dropped out of school early, to work. Yet he always claimed he loved the Depression, because it was so easy to make money then. "Everybody was willing to wheel and deal." And if there was wheeling and dealing, there was a profit to be made, no matter how small. For years he ran a successful business on the side as a 'junk man' recycling anything he could buy cheap during his other endeavours. Many of my earliest memories are of exploring the enormous junk yards of Whalley, a working-class town beside the Fraser River. The scrap piles were like surrealistic scenes out of *Shapes of Things to Come* or the later *Road Warrior* movies — empires of ruin, resembling archaeological digs in a constantly disappearing civilization.

Later, when Father discovered the growing antique market, he used to lament all the expensive brass beds he'd melted down decades before — for only two cents a pound. If he snagged something complex like an abandoned meat cooler, he would pay me to demolish it — setting me loose with a hacksaw and a sledgehammer — a tormented child's idea of heaven. I would blissfully wreck it all, extricating the aluminum and the copper tubing. It seemed wonderfully absurd to get paid for destroying things. Nowadays, of course, it's not worthwhile to junk such objects, and almost everything goes to the land fill.

He had the 'gift' and could talk water out of stones; he could talk birds to sleep. A large, strong man — he weighed 220 pounds with only the one leg — Father worked hard at everything, whether delivering coal or Christmas parcels. He quickly abandoned a temporary career in a mattress factory after he realized all the workers were spitting blood. His father told him: "You get the hell out of there!" This alienated him from punch-clock work, as did a stint tossing rivets in the shipyards.

Working night shifts, he used to stand on the ground with his tongs and pull a white-hot rivet out of the pot, wind up, and hurl it, dripping sparks, several storeys into the air where his catcher snatched it out of the darkness using a bucket, and placed it for the riveter. One night, a catcher wasn't paying attention and was seriously burned by Father's throw. Shortly after that incident, he left the shipyard. He didn't have much stomach for scarring inattentive men.

During the years that followed he drifted into bootlegging potatoes. Throughout the fifties and sixties, when I wasn't at school, he used to take me with him. Bootlegging potatoes consisted of buying cheap spuds off a farmer and selling them door-to-door for less than the stores did, while avoiding the marketing board inspector who could fine us, or seize our truck and spuds. The marketing board was a government monopoly created for the purpose of keeping prices high. It was notorious for unloading rotten spuds on small, independent operators like us when we purchased legal potatoes from them. The trend towards crushing independent working people was once again taking root, after having been beaten back by the anti-monopoly campaigns in the early part of the century.

Since early morning starts were the best way to avoid the inspector, I spent many frosty dawns gazing out from under the canvas flapping on the back of a truck, huddled in a heavy jacket, atop the potato sacks.

Father loved peddling — those morning rides into new adventures every day, the yakking, the challenge of selling to strangers, although the miles of walking and packing hundred-pound sacks took their toll, and his bloody stump would often twitch and 'jump' long into the night. Usually, he worked with a man I called Fat Sid, who in my child's mind I assumed weighed at least three hundred pounds. He occasionally swore at difficult customers and seemed forever grumpy about everything, trudging down the street with his pants so low the crack of his ass showed. I loved Sid. His grumpy exterior concealed a large, unspoken tenderness.

Over the years, there was a parade of helpers, but Sid would always return. Despite different lifestyles, he and Father developed a real affection for each other. I last saw Sid at Father's funeral. He looked diminished, thinner, gentle, and sad; he made me realize how small I must have been in those days to think him so huge.

Another long-term helper we knew affectionately as Crazy Walter. He was a sweet, shy man — indefatigable when he was on his medication, but every couple of years he had to be shipped off to hospital. He told me he needed to get "tuned up" with an electroshock treatment.

Nearing this period, his behaviour would become erratic. It never occurred to Father to fire him because he was going "goofy" again. That was life, and sweet Walter was his helper. The idea of electroshock terrified me, but Walter claimed he didn't mind, though when he returned he was foggy for days.

Walter handled the money and addresses of customers who bought their spuds on credit or 'on the cuff' as we used to call it. Father wasn't much good at math. It was only years later we discovered he'd also been hiding his illiteracy from us. He could skim books and newspapers and figure them out, more or less. It was the writing that escaped him. When this dawned upon Mother he was in his sixties. We teased poor Father so badly that he soon taught himself how to write. We could be savage kin, but in this case, it paid off. He was quite a sight clutching his pencil and paper, outlining letter after stubborn letter until he created a word; then a sentence. After that, there was no stopping him.

Out peddling, there could be hundreds of dollars involved, including the grubstake for purchasing tomorrow's potatoes. One day, in the small town of Squamish, Walter hollered out for Dad to stop the truck, and rushed into a bank. We assumed he had to cash cheques from customers. Later, driving down the treacherous Squamish Highway, Father said, "So what's the take for today?" Walter handed him a deposit slip. He'd put Father's money in a bank account he'd opened in his own name. We had to turn around and go back to the bank, where Father hauled Walter into the manager's office and the two of them explained everything. The money was returned, but Walter grew depressed about misusing Dad's cash like that, and kept trying to leap from the truck along the winding, cliff-hanging highway. Father had to reach over me, clutching Walter by the shirt whenever he saw his twitching hand reach for the door handle. We took him straight to the hospital. After a month of 'tuning up' Walter returned, as good as new.

Another helper, Victor, was more handsome than Steve Reeves, the gorgeous body-builder who became famous starring in Italian sword-and-sandal films, notably in the role of Hercules. I adored

Victor, who was gentle and pretty and strong. We went on a three-day peddling trip with Father's brothers and their helpers to Youbou and Cowichan on Vancouver Island. Victor and I were dropped off at the cabin where we'd all overnight, while the rest of the men sold the load. The cabin was near a bounty hunter's shack. Three dead cougars were hanging from the eaves of his porch. There was an unseemly arrogance about the way he displayed those dead, beautiful animals, so sleek and still.

Victor and I were instructed to bake a heap of chicken for dinner, but Victor discovered a raunchy book and left the cooking to me while he read on the deck overlooking the lake. I managed to cook about six perfect pieces, uniformly dipped and baked and golden brown. I was proud of myself until the ravenous men returned and began screaming and yelling for their dinner. Victor and I caught terrible hell and the men fired up the oven, cooking half a dozen whole chickens in about fifteen minutes, burning the skin black; the meat still bleeding inside. They parked themselves at the oil-clothed table, grunting and smacking their lips, the charcoal sticking to their cheeks and the blood dribbling down their chins. I snuck out the good pieces I'd cooked for Victor and me, and we felt like conspirators eating them. I wanted to be like him, so cool and handsome, but he had a cruel weakness.

He was a heroin addict, and died young from it. Years later, Father told me about visiting him during his last days in a rundown rooming house — how he had no veins left and was belly-popping. He begged Father to shoot him up because he couldn't find uncorrupted veins any more. Father declined. He was very anti-drug. Though Victor's self-destruction by heroin has re-mained with me since childhood, it never stopped me from my own experimentation with mind-altering substances.

Father could talk his way out of almost any tight corner. He managed to get into more than a few of them, like the morning an irate woman with a knife came running down the street after us, holding a large potato cut in half. It was hollow. They were a bad batch — boron deficiency or too much rain on a dry field. We always tried to sell the best spuds. You could never go back after you'd sold rotten potatoes to people. They remembered. Besides, the guilt was not worth a sack of potatoes. Still, if a farmer slipped a bad load past us, we had no choice but to sell them, preferably in a town where we knew we wouldn't return, ever. This always made us feel awful. That's why we ate potatoes daily, to my distress, to keep an eye on the load. If we got burned by a farmer, we didn't return to his barn.

Father never skipped a beat when the woman with the long knife and the hollow potato confronted him. In those days, everybody either boiled their spuds or baked them. No wonder I hated potatoes then. He looked at the lady and said. "Yes ma'am, these are the new breed of potatoes. The hole is where you put your butter when you bake them." She fell for it, and Sid and I curled up laughing in the cab of the truck.

One day, when he returned to a house with change for a twenty a woman had flashed at him after he'd delivered a box of apples, the woman flung the door open and ran terrified past him, startling and puzzling him as she fled down the street. But then he turned back and saw a man with a rifle standing behind the door. Later, Father told us the man's eyes were weird and he was making a giggling sound, a "teeheeheehee" through clenched teeth. Scared, Father fixated on the apples, and he said: "I think I'll take these back." Then he bent down and picked up the box of apples, just inside the door. He turned around, and walked away with his back to the man with the gun, expecting to be shot at any moment. For years we teased him that he was the only man in the world willing to die for a box of apples.

He was so strong he was always surprising us with casual feats of strength — like carrying me and my potatoes along with his own load. I was this frail androgynous creature he had bred, weighing less than a hundred pounds and packing a nearly hundred-pound sack of spuds up five flights of stairs to the storeroom for a Chinese café. I faded near the fourth floor. He grabbed me by my belt, potatoes and all, and half-hauled half-propelled me up that last flight, while he balanced a sack on each shoulder, somehow lurching us up, one grunting step at a time, like a weightlifter seeking one more lift. It was nearly four hundred pounds of weight propelled by one leg, a far-fetched effort he never acknowledged. I think he was afraid of embarrassing me for my inadequacies, which were becoming more obvious as I approached the age when most boys go through puberty.

Perhaps his most notorious peddling trip occurred when he and Sid visited Texada Island. In those days the Texada ferry was an old, converted fishboat. You drove up a ramp on the beach to board it. The islanders were thrilled by our inexpensive potatoes, and the sacks practically floated off the truck. Meanwhile, Father and Sid had noticed all the scrap metal and batteries and junk lying around. Since they were selling out so quickly, they started buying the junk, cheap — because it was inconvenient for the locals to cart to the mainland.

They'd just bought a car motor, and were about to load it into the truck when a car roared up the road. Four big men stepped out, slamming the doors, glaring, playing tough, one holding a rotten spud in his hand. Somebody's wife had been unlucky enough to buy a sack of spoiled potatoes. Instead of asking for their money back they'd decided on trouble. Father and Sid were not the type to be intimidated. They ignored the four posturing men, picked up the motor, which usually required a block and tackle to lift, and heaved it into the back of the truck. The strangers, impressed by this casually performed feat of strength, slowly got back into their car and drove away, without saying a word.

Returning to the ferry, Dad was asked by the ferryman how much the truck was carrying. Father, who always played his cards close, said, "Not much, maybe half a ton." They were probably carrying five tons. The truck was down on its axles. When they drove aboard the ferry the boat tipped, washing its gunnels in the salt chuck. The ferryman went ballistic, screaming that they were going to sink him. The ferry was now so low they couldn't back the truck off. Their only option was to go to sea at that precarious angle, running sideways to the tide so the boat didn't sink from the wash. They made it to the Powell River Dock where a tow truck was waiting to unload them. The ferryman had radioed ahead. The police were also there, and they escorted Father and Sid down the road to the next ferry terminal to Vancouver, and told them to never return again. A few days later a friend of the family sent us the local paper, whose front page headline read: "Peddlers Invade Texada Island."

He was very good at bootlegging, and hardly ever was caught. When he did, it could get exciting. The worst incident occurred when the inspector leapt out of nowhere and into Father's truck, which was stopped at a busy intersection. The man grabbed the steering wheel. Surprised, Father reacted instinctively and hit him so hard he broke his jaw. The police hauled Father off to jail, where he spent the night, building up a good share of righteous outrage over this illegal (the inspectors had no powers of arrest — they needed a police officer for that) and dangerous action by the inspector, before he was finally brought before a judge. After he finished lecturing the judge on the inspector's misbehaviour, Father was released from jail, paid for a day of lost illegal work, and the judge ordered the inspector to apologize to Father for nearly causing an accident, once his jaw healed sufficiently.

That's when I first learned to enjoy the rule of law. Law is a great discipline, alternately hilarious and terrifying. Besides, the judge must have feared a private lawsuit against the inspector, and had sneakily defused Father.

Several years later, the inspector appeared out of nowhere again, and tried to grab a sack of potatoes. For some reason, Father lost his cool, and said: "Here, you want it, you can have it," picking up the hundred-pound sack and hurling it at him, flattening the poor guy. He got busted and fined. After that, he hardly ever lost his temper when confronted by the inspectors.

Another time, a cop caught us cold turkey. He was a big, sardonic man. He looked into the back of the truck and said: "Now what have we got here?" Although Father had larcenous tendencies, he was also honourable, and besides he knew when he was dead in the water. "Potatoes," he said, giving nothing further away. We were facing not only the fine for the illegal potatoes but were also unlicensed for almost everything you could name. The smug officer turned his back to us and opened the trunk of his car. Father picked up a sack of potatoes and dropped it into the trunk. Then he dropped a second one in. Neither man said another word. The cop shut the trunk and drove away.

The police usually didn't want to be bothered with us — they had better things to do; however, since the law declared the inspectors had no power of arrest, not even if we got fractious, which we always did, the cops often found themselves dragged into the mess.

His most legendary tangle with the authorities was started by a notorious inspector who always tried to go head-to-head with Father. I was about fourteen at the time, 'riding shotgun' in this beat-up-looking but skookum panel truck. Father used to go through trucks like most people went through stockings. Some of them might have been rust buckets, but they all had powerful motors.

We were driving down the highway to Langley, packing a full load of spuds. I happened to glance at my rear view mirror and saw the much-feared white car. "We're being followed."

Father downshifted and booted it. Soon we were roaring along a narrow, gravelled lane — throwing up a cloud of dust, approaching one hundred miles an hour as I bounced off the roof. Then the white car was alongside us. He was trying to force us off the road.

This was totally illegal and more dangerous than our speeding, so it offended Father. "Here, hold the wheel," he said, opening his door. I edged over, terrified. My fingers clenched the steering wheel, pale knuckled, keeping the truck's course straight, my foot on the gas. Father, his wooden leg propped on the running board, his right hand locked around the open-windowed door, leaned way out over the hood of the white car — almost in front of the man's steering wheel while both vehicles raced down the gravel road. He shook his fist once, as if he were flexing his bicep, at the wide-eyed inspector. It was so melodramatic it was beautiful.

The terrified inspector braked and spun out, and we were gone.

We headed for my uncle's farm where Father leapt out at the gate and told me to drive the truck up into George's barn. Once it was parked inside I ran down the dirt driveway in time to see both the inspector and a cop car arrive. Father who, long ago had learned the best defence was an offence, called out, as the R.C.M.P. officer emerged from his car, "Officer, arrest this man. He tried to run me off the road!" The cop turned to the inspector, and asked: "Did you do that?"

The inspector admitted to the deed, spluttering that we had a truck full of illegal potatoes. The ludicrousness of this little official trying to force us off the road for untagged potatoes so irritated the cop that he started berating the inspector.

Eventually, settling their differences, they turned towards Father. Since Father had already refused the inspector permission to enter private property without a warrant, the cop asked. "May I go in, then?" Father dragged his wooden leg across the driveway, scratching a line where the farm began. "No, I'm afraid not, officer, this is private property."

After much dickering it became evident they weren't going to see if those potatoes were illegal so the officer and the inspector decided reluctantly to go on about their business, and left, each in opposite directions. We went up to the barn, unloaded all our spuds into George's truck and left. Within a few blocks our empty truck was surrounded by police cars and the smug inspector, who lost his smugness once he realized the truck was empty and Father was threatening to sue for harassment.

Uncle George was selling our potatoes for us, far away.

Father and his brothers had, over the years, divided the lower west coast into territories. We peddled certain districts in Vancouver, along with the Native reserves, and the Doukhobor camp near the Agassiz prison. Numerous Doukhobors resided in that prison due to the Sons of Freedom uprising in the Kootenays, when the young men blew up bridges and burned down the houses of those they believed had sold out the faith. The women often stood naked in front of burning buildings to demonstrate their disdain for the trappings of modern society. After the mass jailings and the seizing of Doukhobor children (who were imprisoned behind chain wire fences in order to be 'educated'), many of the women and the older men, under the leadership of Big Fanny, had trekked hundreds of miles down to the prison where they erected a little shanty town.

Though the camp near where their loved ones were incarcerated didn't last long, I was enthralled. I felt an immediate empathy with the Doukhobors. They might have been the notorious Sons of Freedom, yet they were a marvellous people. The camp resembled an absurd, cubistic slum constructed from recycled pieces of tin, cardboard, cast-off boards, and used windows. It was spotlessly clean. The overweight, big-breasted women recognized my frailty immediately. They would mother me, and drag me into their houses, feeding me chunks of delicious homemade bread and perogies and cream of wild morel soup, while Father wandered around, wondering what the hell had happened to me again. I had a habit of disappearing.

My love affair with Native cultures began then, as well. Father enjoyed peddling in their villages and we were soon friends with the elders of the nearby Salish reserves, as well as several of the more distant communities. To reach one reserve near Agassiz the road followed a small, meandering river which, in the fall, would be writhing with enormous, red-bellied dog salmon, their flesh rotting, pieces of it left behind as they struggled upriver. Masses of eagles clustered in the trees. Others strode along the riverbank, ripping strips of flesh off dying salmon in the shallows. It was a kaleidoscope of colour and death. There were pieces of salmon on the road, on the cliffs. The eagles were imperial, murderous. The salmon squirmed in the mud and the gravel, an orgiastic display of eggs and sperm-milk and rotting, ripped meat.

The local Salish Nation village had lived off the salmon runs for centuries, but except for the dog salmon, the great runs were already fading. Too many of their people were on welfare at the time, and they would buy our spuds 'on the cuff,' and pay later when their cheques arrived. Father was hopelessly generous with his potatoes. He couldn't bear the thought of somebody going hungry, yet at the same time, he usually got his money, though it would often cost more to collect than it was worth.

When I worked with Dad, I was recognized for the strange, damaged creature I was, and taken into the Native homes. They used to love playing long elaborate jokes on me, the humour slow and complex, unlike that of my English ancestors who tended towards slapstick and bullshit, though I have to admit my Italian uncles were pretty good at straight-faced leg-pulling on occasion.

Father could do hilariously impolite send-ups of various cultural voices, from Native to Chinaman to Irishman. Sometimes, with one of the villagers who was a good friend, he'd have side-splitting, 'fake Native,' bunkum conversations that were a combination of Chinook jargon, nonsense, and mushily accented English. I could never figure out who was teasing who. We moved readily into other cultures because Father loved honest dealers and tall talkers, and they were easily found in the Native villages and on the struggling, immigrant farms.

My childhood was spent among great, gentlemanly, hard-working farmers like Mahl I (pronounced 'eye') and Chew Him. After the ancient Chew Him finally retired, handing over his farm to his sons, I once spied him, through a smoky window in a shed behind his house. He resembled a lean mystic, puffing meditatively on his pipe of dreams. There was a lord's grace about the man, perched serenely among his paraphernalia in the little shack.

A few Japanese farmers had returned after the diaspora of World War II which had seen their homes, boats, and vehicles seized and sold. Father liked them because they were good men, but he never forgot the attacks he'd suffered from Japanese street gangs during the thirties and into the war years. They often taunted him about how they'd "take over." They were particularly abusive to Father because his best childhood friend was Japanese — the two of them ended up fighting off both Japanese and English gangs because of their friendship. It got scary for them on the streets a couple of times. Finally, the boy's father heard of the friendship, and beat his son mercilessly, threatening to disown him if he ever caught him hanging around with that white boy again. They still managed to meet briefly, in secret, afterwards; however, the friendship faded. During the war, the young man and his family were rounded up, had all their possessions seized, and were interned in the interior. That was the last Father saw of him.

15

Despite this history, Father gradually found himself working with the few Japanese farmers who returned after this brutal treatment by their own government. They tended immaculate acreages in the Richmond area near Steveston, where they also took up salmon fishing again. Unfortunately, both the charming fishing village of Steveston and the surrounding farmland faced a second diaspora. The developers moved in. The rich earth of Richmond — that sweet, black delta soil, perhaps the best temperate farmland in Canada, was grabbed by the land speculators and paved over with apartment buildings and suburbs — a crime against nature that made me permanently suspicious of politicians and developers. I can still feel that rich earth — driving my fist up to my elbow into the soft, black soil of a field, clutching the roots, and yarding out cabbages as big as medicine balls.

II

Shortly after Father got his first wooden leg he met my mother. In those days, the edges of the Italian and Cockney ghettoes collided on the street where they lived, with the Italians on one side, and the Cockneys on the other. Like Father, Mother, despite her quiet ways, was no slouch in the world of rebellion. Our family loves to tell the tale of a Sunday drive in Comox, when suddenly there was a flashing police light behind the car. Father had a broken tail light. Since they were near their home, Mother's immediate reaction was: "Giv'er guts!" Though he was an expert at dodging the marketing board, he was not about to risk challenging the police over a broken tail light. He could only laugh as he steered the car to the side of the road.

My mother's grandfather was a defrocked priest from the village of Pietragalla, or Stone Rooster, in Basilica, in the south of Italy. He went on to father thirteen children. One of his sons, my grandfather, emigrated to Canada in the twenties, later followed by my grandmother, and gradually, several nieces and nephews, eventually creating a little expatriate community from the village. Grandfather was a card dealer, a grocer, a wine bootlegger, a hotel owner, and an amateur horticulturist on an epic scale. He arrived in America, sailing past the Statue of Liberty, full of dreams. At Ellis Island he signed his landed immigrant papers declaring he wasn't an anarchist, nor intent on the violent overthrow of the American government, had every limb, and wasn't crippled or diseased. That was all it took in those days. There was a relative in New York who, no doubt, stocked him up with sausages and bread and cheese, and he crossed the continent, finally reaching Vancouver, where he lived the rest of his life.

They were a proud, hard-working, and poor family at first, but their hardships didn't compare to the poverty in Pietragalla during that era. My uncles claim they remember listening to the last wolves of Italy when they were young children minding sheep in the hills. The first uncle to emigrate left his young wife and children behind for a few years until he could make enough money to house them decently. His mother kept a strict eye on the family, going so far as to write to complain that his wife was spoiling his children because she'd bought a small dollop of jam to put on their bread one morning.

Though the first years in Vancouver were hard, my grandparents had the Italian peasant knack for eating well and thriving on little. Grandmother bought soup bones for ten cents and concocted minestrones using all the vegetables from the garden, as well as the wild dandelions and mushrooms she'd pick in empty lots. Not much of her history has passed down, perhaps because she died relatively young. She was a tiny woman with remarkable fortitude, but cancer killed her at 51. She died on my mother's 26th birthday. At the funeral, they buried her with her purse, wearing her shoes, because that was the way it was done in Italy.

Many of my family, and those that lived in the streets surrounding them near False Creek, have since died of cancer. I've long suspected there was something toxic emitted from the industries on that creek. When they created Expo 86 the government trucked much of the contaminated soil away and dumped it in the ocean.

Mother has remarkable memories of her childhood in Vancouver — how they ate like kings even as they clambered their way out of poverty.

Our grandparents kept a lush garden, and Grandmother cooked everything from scratch, as well as preserving enough food to feed their family of seven through the winter. In the early days, milk and bread and coal were delivered by horse-drawn wagon, and after they passed Grandfather would take his 'soil' bucket and shovel, and walk the neighbourhood, collecting the manure. I think his steady patience was passed down to Mother, who needed it to keep my father in line. In later years, Grandfather's gladioli would win top prizes at the Pacific National Exhibition. His greatest garden was an extravagant, small acreage in the suburbs that he bought in his later years, a garden I've spent my life seeking. Our vegetable patch on Salt Spring Island is the size of several city lots, yet it seems dwarfed by my memory of Grandfather's landscape, so meticulously kept. He used to lay planks between the beds, and you had to 'walk the plank' in the garden or he got angry. No foot was allowed to compress his soil. Instead of a front lawn there were gravel paths between his prize-winning gladioli beds, all spikey with the lush blossoms.

From the earliest days our extended family was central in our lives. My mother would say about a relative, if an especially bitter internal battle erupted, "but he's family," as if that was the end of the argument. However, being Italian, we had a knack for well-fought arguments, whether at the dinner table or at a card game. I sometimes tease my companion, Sharon, by telling her a good fight helps digest a fine dinner. In those days some ludicrous disagreements and mock quarrels erupted among the pickled peppers and the wine. Dinner was hardly any fun unless someone was in the doghouse; this was very different from Sharon's Scottish family dinners where it seemed the less said the better. My family always had too much to say, and it's been noted I often carry on that tradition.

The family's ascent from poverty to respectability was interrupted suddenly during World War II. One day the police arrived at the door and took Grandfather away, interning him as an enemy alien. Most people assume that only the Japanese were interned during World War II. The history of Canadian racism and xenophobia goes much further than we'd like to admit. Beginning with the First Nations, our maltreatment went on to include Irish, Sikh, and Chinese immigrants. When I was a child one of the worst insults was to be called a D.P. (displaced person) which applied equally to Ukrainians and Italians, and nearly anybody else who wasn't English.

The arrest scarred my family, and had a strong influence on me though I was yet unborn. This outrage from our history, alongside my father's battles with moronic local authorities over peddling vegetables and fruit, cemented my distrust at an early age of the arbitrary actions of governments. Grandfather might not have been an anarchist, but I am, which might explain why I've found myself sucked into the small storms of community politics more than once. Throughout my adult life I've believed in 'tithing,' devoting ten percent of my time to social issues. Sometimes they took up more than ten percent.

Grandfather's only sin was his social nature. Like most Italians, he enjoyed a good party after a hard day's work, and he also supplied the wine for many in the community. The police interned him merely because he was a member of an Italian men's social club. Monstrous police actions never seem to change much. As I write this today, I wonder how many Muslim men are languishing in American jails or being tortured in foreign prisons because of the idiosyncratic decisions of petty Canadian or American officials. I've often thought our family should sue the government for its criminal mistreatment of Grandfather, but they were a little wiser, and took it like stoic Italians who knew that governments can be arbitrary, cruel, and stupid. They preferred getting on with their lives. They were probably right. Obsessions with past injustices and lifelong pursuits of redress can inflame old wounds that need to be left alone to heal. These days, we have a tendency to call picking at scabs a search for 'closure' — a curious concept when you consider the fluid nature of the world. There is no closure. There is only memory and how we live with it.

It didn't take the Italians long to succeed in North America, yet they remained faithful to their roots. The family still owns Grandmother's home in Pietragalla, as well as two fields, which I'm told are very beautiful and have little value, even in the new Italian economic frenzy. Throughout my life, it seems, I've been striving to make beautiful things — gardens, poems, ceramics — all for little money. Maybe I inherited this attitude. My mother, now eighty, recently returned from her second visit in two years to Pietragalla, where she met the children of the relatives who stayed behind. She was feasted with great generosity, and offered endless plates of sheep cheese and olives and wine. Though the lot of the villagers has improved, they are by no means wealthy, yet they eat rich, like most Italians.

The house there is modest, constructed out of stone on a narrow, staired street. It's been abandoned for years. It's not suitable for the new generation. There is no access for a vehicle, and no plumbing. In the old days the family lived in the small rooms above the cellar where the donkey lived. Every morning Grand-mother had to lead the donkey up the stairs from the basement and onto the street and down the street-steps to the fountain for water. She also carried the laundry to the river to wash. It took them an hour to reach their fields. They'd usually bring wine and cheese and bread and salami for lunch, though one aunt recalls that while still a child she often had to carry a big pot full of warm soup on her head to her father and brothers. Grandmother didn't even have a bread oven. She would make a week's worth of bread dough and haul the dough over to the baker — each family was given a specific day on which he baked their bread.

That was one of the first delights of Canada for Grandmother — an oven. Little treats can become big delights when you don't have much. Mother still speaks glowingly of her mama's homemade bread slathered with butter and toasted lightly in the oven. Sometimes her mama would deep-fry the dough in beef fat, and dust it with sugar or a pinch of salt. These were called, *cosa fritte*, fried things. Dessert was often *mustachuel* — dough shaped into a ring, boiled and then baked, the Italian version of a bagel. Grandmother would drizzle icing sugar on them for the kids, but grandfather took his plain because he preferred dipping it in his wine.

Another bread Grandmother would make was called *fuache*. I assume that's a local slang, because I've never found the word in an Italian dictionary. The more common word is *focaccia*. This is flattened bread dough. During tomato season Grandmother would top the dough with basil, oregano, sliced tomatoes, and garlic salt. If there were no tomatoes she would only use the spices. When money was around, she'd spread ground beef and tomato sauce and Romano cheese on the dough — the historic version of pizza. I still make the plain, or the sliced tomato *fuache*.

They usually had two kinds of pasta, one with tomato sauce, and the other called spaghetti *alla allia*, which was mixed with garlic fried in oil and then sprinkled with Romano cheese.

For Christmas, there were *crustels* dipped in diluted honey or icing sugar, and *biscotti*, and the infamous, fart-inducing *lupine* beans. These resemble a cross between a fava and lima bean that you boil lightly before soaking in cold water (usually in a pot in the bathtub with the water barely running — to keep them fresh) for nearly a month before Christmas. Then you drain the beans and put them in bowls and shake some salt on them. To eat the *lupine* you hold it up and squeeze — squirting it into your mouth while retaining the skin which you discard in a dish. This way, you pick up a little of the salt taste. They are dangerously addictive, especially for men, who seem to enjoy the musical side effect. We still devour pounds of them, farting symphonically through Christmas. One of the blessings of poverty is ingenuity, and perhaps no food displays this ability more than the outrageously bitter *lupine* bean converted by poor farmers into a tasty Christmas treat.

At Easter, when times were good, my uncle Giuseppe would buy a goat and kill it. They skinned it by cutting a slit near the foot and blowing into it until the whole goat was swollen. Then they'd open a slit up the belly and the skin would peel off easily. Giuseppe was also particularly fond of sheep's cheese that had been seasoned in a ewe's udder. Once, he asked me to lock up one of my lambs, so it could only drink its mother's milk, and eat no grass or grain. I didn't have the heart for that. I'm sure it would have been delicious, but these are different times. Giuseppe used to regale me with fantastical descriptions of ancient Italian recipes, more than a few unsettling to the modern palate.

My grandfather cherished his honour, and considered himself a respectable bootlegger in the days of my parents' courtship. The selling of wine, with or without the permission of the government, was considered a sacrament, and he was proud of his 'juice of the grape.' The deep, dark wine he made was killer stuff, the product of a tradition that was millenia old. In Italy, since not everyone had the time or skill, each village had its vintners. Here in Canada, these small, home winemakers were labelled bootleggers. Being good Italians, they ignored the government's labyrinthine and often ridiculous liquor laws, and retained their ancient practices. Grandfather was very good at winemaking and he was a popular man in the community. Also, during the twenties and the decade after, there was a

Robin Hood romantic quality to bootlegging. A few smugglers were regarded as heroic buccaneers, and more than one of Canada's wealthiest families began amassing their wealth as bootleggers.

It was only after the Second World War that bootlegging wine started acquiring its seedier qualities, and the family, recognizing the change, quit the business. By then Grandfather had saved enough money to buy a small hotel in the boondocks, from where he began his legal climb into the middle class.

At first Grandfather was horrified by the developing relationship between my parents, and considered my father a gimpy ne'er-do-well, and besides, he was English. But my mother had inherited her dad's independent spirit, so my parents eloped, and she spent a year being shunned by her family. Her sisters and brother had to pretend they didn't see her when they passed her on the street.

Finally, Father and Mother decided this had continued long enough. On a Sunday afternoon, they dressed in their best and knocked on her parents' door. Her little sister was so terrified she wouldn't talk to them but ran for her mama. Italian protocol, despite their unexpected arrival, demanded an invitation to dinner. Following a silent, epic meal, they retired to the living room for cigars and *grappa*. Eventually, everyone relaxed as the molten warmth of shot glasses of *grappa* melted away the icy atmosphere. By the end of the evening, Father was a member of the family. He was soon set up in the wine trade, though his wine was never as good as Grandfather's.

About a year later Grandfather, following another magnificent Sunday dinner, turned to Mother and said. "So, I guess, married to Len, you'll never have to work." This was about his highest praise for a man in those days. It didn't prove true due to the hard times of war and afterward, but Father had passed the grade, despite being one-legged and English. The family was united again, and Father, as it turned out, became more Italian than the Italians.

III

After my birth, the doctor told my mother: "You're going to have to do something about that boy." At least he'd decided I was a boy. Back in 1950 the medical profession had little idea what was wrong with me, and the legacy of that would be decades of pain. I was born an androgyne.

For most of my adult life I was under the impression that I had XXY chromosomes, instead of the 'normal' male XY combination. Even that little snippet of information, I've recently discovered, was incorrect. It's an errant gene, not a chromosome. I don't think any of the doctors really knew much about my syndrome then, except that as I reached what should have been puberty, several thought I was starting to 'present' as a hermaphrodite, with all the social overtones of that term.

I have Kallmann's Syndrome, a rare aberration that causes the hypothalamus to stunt the pituitary gland (the controlling gland for hormones) and can have different complications for every child. In my case I had no male hormones. When I was first diagnosed I was told only one in four million have my syndrome. Recently, I came upon a medical text that said one in ten thousand is born with it. The numbers change, mainly, I believe, because it's a question of whether one has a slight deficiency, or as in my case, the whole shebang. I've been told that with the development of modern technology for genetic testing, my kind have been placed on the 'recommended for termination' list if they are discovered in the womb. I know this is controversial, but I can understand it. The condition is now more understood and some of its worst symptoms can be treated; still, I would not want anyone to feel the pain that I suffered — though now that I've survived more than fifty years in this body, I've grown used to it.

The puberty years were brutal, mostly because I never experienced puberty. My mother, conscientiously remembering what the doctor told her, and aware that I was a 'special one,' brought me in for treatment when I was about fourteen. (The medical records of my early years have disappeared, as if somebody had gone through them, removing the politically incorrect material.) I thought I was a boy, and dressed as one, but my body was completely hairless, even under my arms, and was starting to develop a hybrid carcass that was neither male nor female, although possibly more female, since everyone produces some female hormones, and I guess I was not deficient in that respect. The current term for conditions like mine is 'middlesex.'

Though I had a penis, what the medical profession tactlessly calls a micro-phallus, I guess it could have been mistaken for an enlarged clitoris if you were deeply confused, which a couple of the specialists appeared to be — one told me several times that he thought I might have some latent female organs buried under it all. The doctors, who displayed an impressive ignorance even for that era, operated, to see what they could find.

They sliced open both sides of my groin, and oddly, those six-inch scars have survived, though most of the marks my history has given me have faded. They encountered some vestigial testicles which they yarded down, pierced, and attached by long, tight, black cords sewn cross-legged through the skin and muscles at mid-thigh, so that every time I moved the web would tug on my scrotum (as well as my pierced thighs). I was confined to a wheelchair for a week as I underwent this torturous, barbaric experiment, which they hoped might 'stimulate' me into growing into a man. It didn't work.

The only good thing I can say about those days is that I learned how to be a great wheelchair driver, and could perform wheelies down the length of the ward. I used to have races with the other kids, most of whom were dying from cancer or other diseases far worse than mine. I drove the nurses crazy; they were constantly scolding me and confining me to my room. It was also painful if I fell out of my chair, and sometimes bloody.

My body remained hairless at fifteen, and a growing concern was expressed by some of the specialists about whether I was truly male or female, despite them finding no signs of female genitals. The general opinion fell on the male side, which was correct, even while my body was morphing into a more 'female' form. I wandered lost, and sexless through adolescence, dreaming of being a real human being, or at least a definable one. The doctors gave me a couple of low-dosage shots of testosterone which produced several, wispy, orange hairs in my armpits, and then they lost interest.

I suffered intense headaches. It felt like my skull would fall off, and I was always exhausted and weak, as my small body mutated, growing the identifiable long-boned arms and thighs and the wide hips that should have led to an earlier identification of the syndrome. My skin was velvety, pretty in an unearthly way; but it was a sheet of agony I wore over bones aching like ice against a tooth, and cracking at the joints. During those years I developed 'brittle bone disease' or osteoporosis, which weakened my spine and joints. I grew up expecting pain, assuming it was a natural condition. I learned to take it inside me, swallowing it, metamorphosing proudly, like in the sixties song that declared the more pain the louder the laugh.

Kallmann's can also cause emotional fluctuations. I've done a lot of weeping in my fifty years as well as ramming my fist or head into walls. For a while, following my teens, I used the Chinese characters for deer and dragon as a personal emblem. I was both of these creatures, sometimes simultaneously. These emotional floods can be scary, and from childhood they made me so fearful that I learned how to turn them inward, either by injuring myself or breaking objects I loved. Though I have a high pain threshold I've never enjoyed pain, so hurting myself slowed me up real quick. I had these emotional fluctuations even as an infant, shifting from manic to depressive as if a switch had been flicked. One minute I would be hyperactive, the next near-comatose. This could be dangerous. While an infant, I somehow climbed up on the stove when my mother was distracted, and fell onto the red-hot electric burner. It seared a large series of circles on my stomach, a scar like a target burned into my childhood.

As a young adult, when I was finally diagnosed, I was treated with regular, high-dosage testosterone injections, which I'll have to take for life. The shots increased my emotional floods in the early years of the injections, and my passions can still catch me off-guard even today, though I'm now better at recognizing and dealing with them, as well as slowing down with age. These hormonal up-heavals are well-known and documented today due to the number of body-builders using illegal steroids. Gyms are rife with tales of them going into unpredictable steroid or 'roid' rages. Over the years, my 'roid' rages have lessened, which is a relief. However, before I was diag-nosed, I had no idea what they were and they were deeply troubling. Since I wasn't taking testosterone as a child, it's evident that more than this hormone causes those floods, though it did noticeably en-hance them once I began the injections. My behaviour also disturbed the people around me. A teacher beat my hands with a leather strap thirty-six different times in grade six for bursting into fits of weeping in class. The teacher, our school principal, an old-fashioned bullet-headed ex-football player, decided he was going to "make a man" out of me and stop my blubbering. He could never fathom that just looking at the ethereal beauty of the world through the classroom window was enough to drive me to tears, nor did I have the ability to explain this to him.

Since his strappings failed to stop my crying, he decided to con-sign me to a school for what they called the 'retarded' in those days. The officials arrived with a battery of intelligence tests, and after they were finished, they neatly folded everything up, gazed silently at me for a while, and went away.

It was a decade later that I learned one of the side-effects of Kall-mann's Syndrome is either mental retardation or, very differently, an early-maturing mind (not necessarily a more intelligent one). To-wards summer, I was told by another, more sympathetic teacher that I'd blown bullet-head's tests off the map. According to the results I should have been graduating from university in some subjects. The principal, a stubborn man with his own agenda, continued strapping me for my outbursts, especially after the time I abruptly pulled my hand back and he whacked himself on the thigh with his pebble-grained, maroon-leather strap. Enraged, he practically ribboned my hand. But the balance of power had shifted invisibly. It dawned on me that he could beat me but he couldn't change me. I remembered my tally of hits as if they were a gunslinger's notches in his gun. I still wept in class for no apparent (to him) reason, though I never cried when he strapped me. This drove him crazy with anger.

I got wilder. I started running away. Once, my father gave me $1.35 to buy gas and mow the lawn. I threw the gas can in a ditch, and wearing a thin coat, hitchhiked to the interior. The weather was mild and the grass was growing in Vancouver, but it was thirty below in Princeton. At a roadside restaurant in the wilderness, they fed me and let me stay in a cabin in exchange for chopping wood and doing chores. They must have felt sorry for me. I was nearly fifteen but could have been mistaken for an eleven-year-old girl, and I wasn't talking about where I came from. It took me three days to reach Penticton, where a kindly driver who didn't believe my far-fetched and changing story about relatives in Montreal used a clever subterfuge to turn me in to the police, and thus prevented me from joining the circus, which was my real intention. (I finally did join a circus for a brief period, but that was three years later.) I ended up spending a night in jail, without my shoelaces and belt, weeping hysterically, until the police booked me into a foster home. And then, in those days of old-fashioned justice, after they tracked my family down (I still wasn't talking much but they got my name and address out of me, somehow), merely placed me on a bus, instructing the driver to not let me out of his sight until I reached Vancouver and my waiting parents.

My father was impressed by my disappearance, and used to brag about how dangerous it was to send me out for gas.

Following this incident, at a family party that grew raucous, while my father was once again crowing about my travels, one of my uncles, who'd had too much to drink, decided to eat several of my prize-winning tropical fish, swallowing them whole, alive. That's when I decided, like every teenager, that I would never be like my family. In my mind I was already gone — down the long, feral road out of childhood that I'd eventually follow. I used to sit across the dinner table, feeling superior, glaring at my father. It must have been terrible for him, but he held his temper most of the time. I did not truly reconcile with him for years, and it took me three decades to realize how much like him I am, and that inheriting his defiant spirit is probably what saved my life.

I've always had eccentric, complex, technicolour dreams. I often wonder if the Kallmann's is behind them as well. They were especially harsh during my late childhood and early teen years. I feared sleep for the nightmares it would bring. The combination of sleepless nights and the low energy levels caused by my syndrome left me constantly exhausted. No wonder I was so weepy. The situation climaxed one night when I was suffering a particularly terrifying nightmare. I was being chased by a gorilla through tall yellow grass. It was going to catch me any second. Then, I saw an iron bar lying on the ground.

I sprang above that grass like a samurai on speed, the bar slung back overhead, bringing it down with a crunch on the skull of the onrushing gorilla. That was it — one of the most powerful moments in my young life — I could change my dreams.

Near the age of thirteen I encountered a creature stranger than dream monsters. I was alone in the house. It was night. I walked into my bedroom and there was a face looking in the window, the same face all the 'abductees' describe — the alien king. It had the high forehead and the big eyes, its smooth skin was a greenish brown. My heart in my throat, I fled the room. After several minutes, I couldn't stand not knowing if I'd just imagined the vision, and returned to the room. It was still there, gazing at me, wide-eyed, serene in the eerie silence. I stood frozen at the door, and it seemed like forever until I screwed up the courage to back out of the room. The oddest thing about this encounter was that the window was on the second floor. There was nothing for the alien to stand upon. When I went around to our kitchen extension, which had a window overlooking my bedroom, there was nothing there. I returned to my room. Gone.

This incident allowed my hyper-neurotic mind to convince myself that I was alien seed, abandoned on Earth by my 'real family.' My father and mother would have been mightily im-pressed by this conclusion, so I never told them. Over the decades, in books, I encountered other writers who met a similar alien in the window.

It's like a thread running through the lives of many artists, from Jack Kerouac to P.K. Page. I often wonder if this vision is a marker of the sensitive mind, the one that has undergone what Margaret Atwood called "the click" — the sea-change that turns women and men into artists.

I took my first LSD when I was fifteen. And I saw Blake's grain of sand, only it was riding rocket ships and lived inside my gaudy, paisley shirts as I listened to Jim Morrison's sexy voice crackling out of a battery-powered radio while I log-danced down the driftwood-heaped beaches of the coast. I saw a lot more aliens, but they came out of the sugar cube or the blotter or the micro-tab. In my outrageous costumes I appeared at all the 'Be-ins' and snuck into clubs, occasionally disguised as a woman, less likely to be questioned about my age if they were strict with their liquor licenses. I loved the amoebic light shows and the excitement of the bands who thought they were going to change the world: Country Joe and the Fish, Big Brother and the Holding Company, with Janis Joplin at the Retinal Circus. I saw The Who when they were the support band for Herman's Hermits, and was hypnotised by Keith Moon's histrionics at his drum kit. That was the first time I saw a crowd rush a stage. They hit it with a sickening crunch. Then there was Arthur Brown in '68, with his doctorate in philosophy, prancing around the stage, his head in flames, declaring himself the god of hellfire. The final Doors concert in Vancouver confirmed everything I believed, despite critics claiming it was one of their worst performances. During the last song Jim Morrison stood defiantly on the stage while being swamped by screaming women, many ripping their blouses off. He would fall under the heap of squirming bodies and then pop out while the cops hurled them aside as he sang about 'the end.' I agreed with him completely. Considering my condition, part female, part male, all strange, I fell into the sixties like a fly into shit.

No one had told me the world could go this far. I was enthralled. I met Buddha and Christ and Tolkien's hobbits, which is all laughable now, but I also met something more — the knowledge that the world could be seen differently.

As my teen years progressed, my escapes from home became more common. I was a lost, young dog — sneaking out, going where I shouldn't go, and experimenting with drugs. I was sexually assaulted several times. It took me years to recover from the shock of those incidents, especially an ugly one in the forest near my school. Tree stumps have always held a fascination for me because of what stepped from behind one. My parents had said it was dangerous out there, and they were right. I never told them about these traumas, mostly because I was going where I shouldn't be going. Now, looking back, I find myself feeling sorry for the creeps. They were pathetic and sad. They needed treatment, not prison.

I was pretty. I was weird. The strange ones could smell me in a crowd. Everywhere I went I was assaulted. And I went everywhere because I was burning. The assaults lasted for more than a decade, starting when I was around thirteen. I was molested in the bathroom of a decrepit theatre during the intermission in a *Bomba* movie, and constantly in strangers' cars because I was a compulsive risk-taker and hitchhiker. A young woman with an enormous chest used me under an old bridge in one of the now-buried ravines of Vancouver. I didn't object, hypnotized by the tactile nature of her pneumatic breasts, though my skin was so hypersensitive I hated being touched. I inhaled all of it. I thought this was life.

That's when I started reading addictively. At first it was trashy boy's stuff and animal stories, *Big Red* and *Bring'em Back Alive*, but the books took me outside my body. Unfortunately, my father, if he caught me reading, assumed I had nothing to do and would give me that little forked-stick-thingy and make me weed dandelions from the lawn. I considered this a bizarre punishment. For him, reading was only something you did when there was nothing on TV, and I suspect he unconsciously felt threatened by books due to his lack of formal education.

Since my parents were not shy about work, they began their climb into the middle class, guided by Mother's clever handling of money. Once Father earned money he had little idea how to bank it. They were a good combination. They bought a house for $2,000 during an era when everyone thought buying a home was a crazy idea because rents were so cheap. They had to use apple boxes for furniture. They eventually bought their first new house in a suburb when I was a teenager, and soon installed a pool table in the basement.

I quickly got the hang of the table. I developed a talent, and began frequenting the local pool halls. In one of them, the kindly owner, confined to a wheelchair, took me under his wing, and would let me read in the back for hours on end. Since my father, raised in the rough East End, considered the pool hall a natural place for a young man, he didn't object.

Everything worked out perfectly, except this was also the biker's hall, and that's where I started hanging out with the Hell's Angels.

They decided I was a freaky hoot, and I became their unofficial mascot — their book reading, androgynous, pool-playing wizard of a kid. They loved it when a tough new biker rolled into town and swaggered up to the money table for a challenge match. They'd tell him he had to play me first. This would involve a few grandiose objections and curses and strutting, but they were adamant. Finally, I would rise from my pile of books in the dark at the back of the hall, my book table illuminated only by my reading lamp; then I'd slink up to the felt and "whup his ass," as the Angels used to proudly exclaim. For them, every performance was a source of amusement.

I knew they were a crooked, mean bunch — a few later ended up in the front pages of newspapers for their misdeeds — yet they treated me with care and generosity. And they'd buy me a hot cubanette sandwich after I won.

I became very good at pool and eventually, older and living on my own, I joined the crowd at Pender Billiards, where legendary players with flamboyant nicknames like Darrell the Cowboy (who later taught me the aesthetics of the racetrack), Eric the Englishman, and Big Bill played all-night high-stakes money games with anyone foolish enough to challenge them. They frequently skinned the pretentious crowd at Seymour Billiards, including a young Cliff Thorburn. This was before his skill peaked and he won the Canadian championship, which Big Bill also won later. I thought the quiet Englishman was the best player. However, something happened, and he never entered the world of tournament snooker, at least as far as I know. One afternoon I watched him running a perfect game of snooker, before he caught himself in a corner and had to take a yellow instead of the black. The silence in the building roared in my ears as he slid his way down that table. I wasn't good enough to shine the shoes of these players, yet I learned a little about the beauty of skill and self-control from them.

In my teens, woofing whatever I could drink or drop or smoke, I was becoming wilder at home, rebelling against everything. Since I'd fixated on Father, he became my enemy, much to his surprise because he was a likable guy, and considered himself just that. So it got rough, like the night I chugged a twenty-sixer of vodka on a bet. I had serious alcohol poisoning and was hallucinating by the time I arrived home. In the ensuing scuffle Father tried to sober me up by sticking my head under the cold water in the kitchen sink as my fingers wrapped around the handle of a knife lying on the counter. This annoyed him. "What! You wanna use knives now?" And he shoved me under even harder while I struggled — though at least I was smart enough to drop the knife. I still have a slight ridge in my eyebrow from where I bounced off the tap. It makes me remember those troubled years and the love for him I eventually allowed to grow despite my worst efforts.

I might have been all screwed up, but I could move like grease on a grill, and I've got a tongue like a whip. The two of us would have confrontations that resemble rooster dances, or perhaps more accurately, bear baiting. I'd be floating around him, wigging out, while he turned slowly, anchored on his wooden leg. Then I'd be gone. He'd have to throw things at me — tool boxes, radios, gumboots — whatever he could reach to slow me up and hold me down, because otherwise I would be history, out the door, run away again. Years later, when we had a family quarrel over a few lines I'd written about our misadventures, he suddenly blurted out. "I never beat you!" To which I replied. "Well, you didn't use your fists." And he hadn't either, though a lucky backhand could drive me across the room if he caught me on the run. "Well that's that, then," he said. His honour satisfied. And I suddenly realized how much it had injured his self-respect when he mistakenly thought I'd accused him of "beating" a kid (instead of trying to discipline a juvenile menace). Looking back on all our fights now, I feel guilty for the violence I goaded out of him. In the end, though, I think we both gave as good as we got, which is probably the best either of us could have asked for during those traumatic years.

I grew stubborn about my physical inadequacies and tried to overwhelm them. The other children, male and female, used to tease me that I ran, or threw a baseball, like a girl — an ugly insult in the school yard — so I attempted toughness. If I got in a fight I would never stay down on the ground, the 'honourable' way to close a fight. I kept on getting up until I physically couldn't or until my opponent tired of pummelling me. Then I tried gymnastics. I was awkward and clumsy because of my distorted limbs, yet my obdurate nature pushed me to my limits. I could do full backwards somersaults from a standing position. They were sloppy, but I accomplished them, and since my joints were rubbery I could achieve astonishing yogic contortions. I became a little twitchy about gymnastics after a backward somersault off a diving board at the local pool. I went straight up and straight down, hitting my head on the board. I woke up at the bottom of the pool. It was eerie, and beautiful in an odd way, suddenly regaining consciousness in the clear blue water. Kids swam and played overhead. I lurched, choking, to the surface. The lifeguard was looking around fearfully, wondering what that noise (the crack when I'd hit the board) had been, as I reached the pool's edge, my head hammering with pain.

At seventeen, I met my second biggest influence after my family. He was a Bella Bella Indian with a Master's degree in Classics who later went on to be a Chief in his village — my grade 11 English teacher, Cecil Reid. He was also an amateur boxer, or so he told us after he showed up with a black eye on a Monday morning. He recognized the unconventional edge in me and another student, Mario Blasevich.

Mario wrote short stories like dreams. For a while we were close friends. Years later, Mario got caught by a storm, summiting the third highest mountain in the Himalayas, and they had to carry him down, frostbitten, in a basket. He lost the tips of several fingers and toes.

Mr. Reid brought us wads of photocopies because the textbooks were useless: the erotic lyrics of D.H. Lawrence, the poems of Wallace Stevens, the plays of Arrabel, and the first translation into English of Bertolt Brecht's electrifying *Mahagonny*, the City of Nets. "O show me the way to the next whisky bar. If we don't go now, we must die. We must die." He brought in the bad boys, the *poètes maudites*, Corbière and Laforgue. Then one day, he showed up beside my desk with a book and said: "So you think you're tough, eh? Read this." It was Jean-Arthur Rimbaud. When I read his "Wild Child" I suddenly understood there was a different way. By then I was borrowing hubcaps, and sometimes cars. A joy-riding firecracker, I was going down bad roads too fast. That book arrived just in time.

And thus I was 'saved' at a faceless high school in the suburbs of Vancouver, deep in the heart of this sad, shallow culture of ours. I still have the Penguin prose translation of Rimbaud's collected poems, rebound by hand several times during the past thirty-five years, plus all the photocopied texts given to me by Mr. Reid during the two years I studied under him. I carry the Rimbaud with me whenever I travel, like a talisman, a reminder of who I was and where I want to go. With Rimbaud, at first, it was the lifestyle along with the poetry. Now that I have survived into my fifties, I prefer the poetry.

There were a few close calls along the way.

I burned him, my teacher, unfortunately, in my pyrotechnical race for oblivion. He had to finally throw me out of his class, as did seven of the eight other teachers, at one point or other, during my last year of school. Only the unflappable art teacher could tolerate me. Then I decided I wanted to go to university. This was tricky since I had failing or near-failing grades in several subjects and was constantly being evicted from classes. I discovered they were legally bound to give me the scholarship exams if I de-manded them. For my presumption, and maybe because I was so feckless, my teachers assigned me brutal grades for their segment of the scholarship score, working on my past history and the assumption I was the one most destined to fail. I realized I'd better read the course textbooks. It ended up, luckily, that the exams were a joke, and I learned I received a stratospheric score in English. Someone also told me I'd received the highest grade in History (of all things) in the annals of the school. I must have been on acid when I wrote that test. No doubt the premature mental development of my syndrome also helped. I can remember the teachers, afterwards, coming out of their rooms to stare silently at me as I marched down the hall to collect my scholarship papers. I only received second-class because their predictions crashed my score. Still, it was enough to pave my way into university, even if I was near-destitute. My parents, despite my nuttiness, and my refusal to speak to my father half the time during this testy period, gave me whatever money they could afford, and I went to work cooking hamburgers and living off my pool cue. I was going to get an education at last, or so I thought.

I fell into Rimbaud's alchemical world through his poem "Voyelles." Alchemy, 'the great work,' was not only about turning lead into gold, but about turning mud into a man. I read only books that were at least a hundred years old, searching out ancient texts in my quest to become a man. The university proved to be useless, except for a few brilliant professors like Robin Blaser, Jerald Zaslove, and a wonderful Spanish multicultural-studies teacher whose name I've now forgotten, but my early alchemical and hermeneutic writings convinced her I was off the deep end.

I was.

I also got into my share of trouble at the university, sometimes with my new business partner, Allan Safarik. We'd started a publishing house in that brash, typical way of young hotheaded students, because we didn't like what was being published by the regular publishers. We had some great times together, though we eventually quarrelled over Blackfish, and I left it in his hands.

Typical of the offbeat and sometimes amusing trouble we often found ourselves in was an incident that occurred when, for who knows what reason, Safarik and I attended a Marxist-Leninist Party of Canada rally at a university lecture hall. The hall was packed, which surprised us. But this was the end of the sixties; so people were open to anything, including Maoists. It was the usual harangue. We soon grew bored and were trying to figure out how to politely leave when a voice shouted. "Halt, there's a fascist in our midst!" This almost made me giggle, and if I remember correctly, Safarik, in a sudden moment of paranoia, thought at first they were talking about us. In those days we couldn't be termed fascists by any means. Especially me. I was a rabid anarchist and, out of eccentricity, carried a business card declaring my membership in the I.W.W., the International Workers of the World, the 'Wobblies' — the last great romantic revolutionary workers' organization of America. We realized that all heads had turned towards a lonely figure seated in the middle of the auditorium. It was Stanley Cooperman, legendary poet, lecher, and decadent. He was also a Zionist, which didn't go over big with this crowd.

I always loved Stanley. He was full of gusto until his past caught up with him and he committed suicide. He rose to his feet, proud, surveying the angry crowd, and said: "Whaaa? I just came to hear your side of the argument. You should be grateful." Or something like that. This approach didn't go over well among that pack of brainwashed lunatics. With a roar they turned on him, and Stanley was lifted bodily into the air, fists flailing, as they attempted to eject him from the hall.

While we were no fans of Stanley's outrageous right-wing politics, this treatment went against our sense of fair play and we waded into the mélée, which became a general brawl. We were hopelessly outnumbered and unable to protect Stanley. The only thing I can say in the Maoists' favour is that they were such incompetent fighters, nobody got hurt. The three of us were turfed out into the hall. Then it got ugly because one of the Maoists finally connected and hit Stanley, knocking him to the floor, which also proved to be a fatal mistake, for at that moment the university football team happened to be returning to their classes after a workout. You may imagine the reaction of these right-wing jocks when they saw one of their professors being knocked down by an angry rabble under a Maoist banner. A couple of players picked up Stanley and dusted him off while the rest descended on the mob of lightweight, scrawny politicos. It was a riot in all senses of the word. The football team cleaned their clocks and there were Maoists running for cover everywhere. Safarik and I supported Stanley and tried hard not to laugh at this unexpected conclusion to the affair.

I eventually recognized I was learning more in the cafeteria and the library than in the classroom. I kept dropping acid, and soon I found my anger drifting towards the mean streets. My world at this point was a hybrid of drugs, the library, radical politics, the seedy life of the East Side, alchemical texts, and pure, sexless, androgynous desire. I continually placed myself in harm's way, although I couldn't abide having my burning skin touched. I was an odd meal — one portion like a paranoid woman who'd been stalked, another portion my father's gusto and *élan*, and the final portion the analytic mind of my mother.

The headaches and the manic-depressive states were fierce. I lived for dark rooms. I skulked about the university, drifting like a ghost through the library, homeless much of the time because I often refused to go near my parents and was usually broke, so I lived out of a locker and slept in a sleeping bag in the rotunda at the university, or on the streets, or with whoever would take me in. I wore typical sixties clothes, an abstract-embroidered poncho and magenta bellbottoms, pink peasant's shirts with frills down the front and on the ends of the sleeves.

I read everything. Books were also a drug — a way out, as well as in. I learned to love the dream of books. If nothing else in my life, I have become a good reader. I had no one to discipline my studies, and still don't. I will usually read several books at once, biographies, natural histories, novels, physics, astronomy, poetry — all mixed up into a complex soup. Comic books, newspapers, cereal boxes, I read like some people breathe. It's an obsessive behaviour — an amateur psychiatrist might tag it a need to escape the world, a variation on whisky. Myself, I know I read to enter the dialogue of the world, to confront the forces beyond my skin, and thus learn what is under my skin. I read to live.

IV

And then at twenty, during one of my usual, useless visits to a specialist, I let drop a comment, and the doctor did a double-take. I had given him, at last, unknowingly, the key to my condition. He was talking about pleasure, sensual reactions, and asked how I reacted to the smell of coffee in the morning. The mind is a crazy creature. As soon as I heard the question, I realized for the first time in my life: "I can't smell." At least not in the normal way that people smell, which is probably why it took me twenty years to recognize this absence. It's called ansomia.

He smiled triumphantly and, typical of the doctors of his time, said nothing. I needed a "few tests." Taking my slip of paper to the appointed room, I found myself being strapped down, with an X-ray machine put to my head. I was proud and stubborn, and showed little emotion, but inside I was exploding. Suddenly, everything was clear. It was inside my head! They were checking out my pituitary gland — my poor, damaged, third eye.

The shock of this soon had me whimpering. It was inside my head! Then they admitted me into the hospital for further testing, which is where they finally realized I was producing no testosterone. I was a near-perfect androgyne. That's when I got it into my head I was one of the homunculi; the miniature, sexless man of the alchemists — Lully and his companions questing for their great work — a man in the process of being born into his true form, the ghost in between; the creature so exquisitely defined by the alchemist Aureolus Philippus Theophrastus Bombast von Hohenheim — Paracelsus — a philosopher both portentous and foolish simultaneously.

A few days after admission into the hospital, I was downstairs having a coffee with Allan Safarik. There was a fellow from the Italian cleaning crew seated at a crowded table next to us, an ugly, brutish man, hairy and massively eyebrowed like a sexist caricature. He gave me a jab in the shoulder and asked loudly: "Are you a man or a woman?" The rest of his crew burst into laughter.

Although I'd been asked that question often before, this time I lost it completely, and ran away, hysterical. Safarik, I was told later, flew into a rage, and started using the cafeteria chairs for soccer balls. The cleaning crew, recognizing they were in deep trouble, evacuated. I ended up weeping my way down the hospital halls, until finding my room, where I cowered on the floor behind my bed. The nurses gave me a sedative. It was an eventful night at Vancouver General Hospital.

My 'feminity' was always a dicey subject in the family, and difficult for my father. A few years earlier, though he never discussed my condition (only Mother had shown the strength previously), he asked if he could see. I dropped my pants in front of him and he just sat in his easy chair, staring; then he turned his face away without saying a word. That was crushing. It was also harsh for him, and I think he feared his genes had caused my condition, as if he had failed me in some male way, when actually the syndrome came from the Italian side of the family.

Meanwhile, the doctors continued treating me like a frog that needed dissecting.

If I were to hold any grudge in my life, I'd hold it against that clique of specialists who treated me during those years with arrogant, thoughtless cruelty. Sometimes they'd bring a cluster of interns to my hospital room to look at and touch my body "to see what you are like" — not considering that having dozens of strangers grope your genitals every day can be a little demeaning. They would do tasteless things like walk me down the hall for a "test," and without warning, direct me into a classroom of medical students where the students would ask me dumb, embarrassing questions about my lack of a sex life, what it felt like to be an androgyne, what I thought about coffee, and how it tasted without being able to smell. For various reasons, my inability to smell fascinated them. Like all stories, however, ansomia is more complex than it sounds.

Because I can't smell, my sense of taste seems to have hypersensitized. Scientists tell us that a lack of smell means a lack of taste.

This is not exactly true. I have such a distinct sense of bitter, salt, sweet, sour, and *umami* (the fifth taste), that it can be hard to live with. Strong flavours launch me into a feverish sweat. My friends often ask me to identify spices or foods because my hypersensitivity is well known. Yet certain flavours completely escape me. Despite my inability to smell, I can still taste the air. I flick my tongue like a snake to pick up delicate scents, whereas outrageously nauseous scents for others will slide right past me — though usually, if something is in the air I can detect it. It's embarrassing to be caught licking the air, so I don't do it unless I'm with friends or I can conceal my behaviour.

To a certain extent, the behaviour of the doctors is justifiable. I should be the first to appreciate the need for research on syndromes like mine. It was the insensitive way they used me that was so distasteful, the disregard for my emotional state, which was already precarious. After all, not only was I suffering the emotional roller coaster of Kallmann's Syndrome, but I was also facing all those curious glances on the street, and the whole North American psychosis about femininity in men during an age when you could (and did) get beaten up for looking like me. This was especially difficult for me since my stubborn side had grafted onto the psychedelic revolution. I was the second 'boy' in school to wear his hair long, in defiance of those who were dragging longhairs into back alleys and shaving them. We fought for our hair in those days, one of the reasons why it's amusing to see that the modern version of being hip means shaved heads.

For the specialists I was a subject they could write advanced papers about, a rare freak of unknown qualities. I was good business. Then came the day I snatched my records when my doctor was out of the room, searching for more colleagues he could display me to — a common ritual. A letter in my file said: "Thank you so much, Doctor . . . for introducing me to this very interesting monster." The word monster has resonated for me ever since, and I wrote a chapbook of prose poems called *Monster: An Autobiography*, in which I portrayed myself as a monstrous swamp creature on the rampage. Due to the incident with the letter and the sequence of molesters I encountered, I've always been curious about the nature of creeps and serial killers — the monsters of society. Perhaps the minds of some among us who've been injured are stamped with a need to understand the psychology of those who injure, yet I've never found it in myself to hate those who treated me cruelly. I only want to know why, and so I've returned often to the subject in my writing.

I was suspicious of doctors for a long time. Thankfully, they don't talk that way any more, at least not on paper, or in public, and over the last two decades I've been lucky enough to encounter a kinder, more sensitive, new generation of specialists, who also know a lot more about my condition.

And thus they ended up injecting me full of testosterone and casually sent me on my way without any psychological aid or even a follow-up to see how I was doing. The initial shot was so strong my tiny organ developed an erection that lasted for eight days. I hid out in my basement, a boarding-house-room next to a roaring furnace. Soon, I was screaming in pain because it hurt so much after the first hours. I might have been "tiny in every way" as one doctor said, but it still drove me mad with agony.

That's how they started making me into a man, how I began 'growing' into my inheritance.

I gradually learned to forgive the callous actions of the doctors, but in those days I was twisted up after the specialists got through with me. The last straw occurred when I asked one of the doctors what my syndrome meant, what kind of future I would have. He said: "Your kind has no history of living beyond forty." Then he casually went on with his note-taking.

Rocket ship time. Only now I was fuelled by straight shots of testosterone. I was a menace to the universe, and nuclear powered, too. Sexually charged, by what later turned out to be excessively large injections during that period, hungry to live and haunted because I was going to die young, I decided I might as well try everything. I did. I tried everything — or close to it.

V

I advanced on the roughest districts of Vancouver. I became a hormone-fuelled human tornado immersing myself, off-and-on, in the floating world of the street for nearly two years. I was an exotic dish leaning against the lampposts on Granville Street. Those days remain so troubling that, nearly thirty years later, I still find myself unable to talk or write about them in detail. The doctors tell me the physical damage I did to myself then will, in all likelihood, kill me eventually.

I became a wandering poet, dropping out of university for the life of the road and adventure. When I was twenty years old I was 5'7" and weighed 114 pounds. Thanks to the testosterone I grew to 6' tall and weighed 147 pounds by my thirtieth birthday. Now, in my fifties, I'm back down to 5'10". The bones seem to have compressed or shrunk, and are crumbling at the joints, likely due to the osteoporosis I developed in my untreated teen years. The testosterone has made me wide-faced, outrageously hairy, and I keep packing on the bulk. I currently weigh 230 pounds. Over the years I have metamorphosed into a creature resembling my childhood biker pals.

When I was young, my father used to set his chest on fire with a cigarette lighter. This bit of semi-macho goofiness became a family tradition for a while. There'd be contests among the men to see who could make the biggest whoosh. At first, since I was hairless, I was out of the game, but as the testosterone shots took hold in my twenties and I could shave at last, I grew so hairy I'd win hands down. Due to the forest fires I could create on my chest the competitions almost grew dangerous, so they became more infrequent. But Sharon, my companion, loves it yet, and sometimes, when we've both had too much Scotch, the devil in her cons me into taking off my shirt and setting my chest on fire — for old time's sake. It's as funny as hell watching how people react to this — especially the first time they see it. The men always shake their heads and grin ruefully, while the women find it hysterical. The stink and the sudden blue-green crackling flames light up their eyes. And besides, it keeps the awful hair growth down. Sometimes I discover body hairs four inches long, and I feel like I'm being testosterone-injected back into an animal existence from a previous life. So I submit myself to Sharon and our big scissors. It's another hapless job she gets stuck with. I stand with my joined palms reaching for the sky, listening to the click of the blades.

It's daunting to live with such a constantly morphing body — capping that with the natural progression of age. I often feel like I'm in a cave looking out a window, or in the cab of a truck, perched above an engine that never will run right, all the cylinders firing in the wrong order. But it's been fascinating witnessing the various sexual colours of the spectrum.

Almost a decade ago I was chairing a Writer's Union of Canada panel when it collapsed into an acrimonious quarrel over discrimination, racism, and sexism — the usual stuff that intellectuals can get worked up about in our era. I found myself drawn into a confrontation with the fine novelist, Audrey Thomas.

I think I made a sympathetic remark about knowing what it's like to suffer. Audrey retorted from the back of the auditorium: "Brian, you can never know what it's like to suffer the way women have." To which I said: "You might be surprised." This annoyed Audrey, who I consider a friend, and she exclaimed: "Oh come on, give us a break." Verbal sparring matches often erupt between writers on contentious issues, so I didn't think much about it. However, to my amusement, I found myself being booed by the strident faction seated a few rows in front of Audrey. I was a hair away from launching into my abused history right there on stage.

It was one of the few times I've been smart enough to keep my mouth shut. Besides, I've never given much credence to today's cult of victimology. So I let it go, but it reaffirmed the knowledge that my syndrome has given me — assumptions and cultural conditioning betray our real connection with the world. Nothing is what it seems, yet we use our conditioning, from whichever point on the political circle we receive it, to justify our daily lives. Even when I was supporting someone — in this case, Audrey — I could still end up the outsider for the booing cluster seated in front of her, clutching their dogmatic agenda.

I've learned over the years how to live with being treated cruelly for the way I looked — either too female or too male — yet for me, this moment was a real turning point. I suddenly felt free — the pain of those early years had faded. For the first time I began to talk about my condition. Up until then, perhaps only a few very close friends and lovers knew of it. I didn't feel ashamed any more.

I can think of better ways of achieving cathartic moments than being shredded by a pack of angry feminists, but we can only accept our glories as they come, or as Nietzsche's motto proclaims: *amor fati* — love your fate.

Before I finished my tumultuous twentieth year, I ended up in Vancouver General again. This time I arrived with an overdose. I must have had an awesome reputation in the hospital in those days. I had been out on the street, looking for mescaline and got tangled up in one of those odd transactions that always seem to happen in the underworld. I ended up buying sixteen hits of Windowpane LSD. I was with a young prostitute friend who was semi-wired on heroin. Because I still had a little cash left, she was on my case big time. She wanted me to buy her some 'junk,' but I wasn't interested. She kept pestering me. So I did one of my famous space-outs: "Okay, if you want to drive me away; then watch me go." I swallowed all sixteen hits of the Windowpane in front of her.

I'm told the acid in the sixties was very different from the acid today — more pure, the dosage stronger. And Windowpane was the best of the best. One hit could make you cling to the walls as they wriggled out of your grasp. Guided by the yellow people (even their eyes were yellow), I was taken through the rainbow dimension to meet God — because I couldn't give them the right word, the one that would save me. As soon as I realized I didn't know the word, my universe collapsed. I still can't remember what God said to me about my failures when I faced Him. I don't think it was nice. For that matter, I can't remember what God looks like either. It would be nice to know.

All this happened downtown at Love's Skillet Café on Gran-ville Street. Apparently, it took two squad cars and an ambulance to haul me to the hospital. For years afterwards, I was recognized by all the street kids, who'd decided I was the king of the acid-heads on the strip. Apparently, I'd caused some ruckus.

In the Psychiatric Ward, a cop sat at the foot of my bed, transcribing my ranting in case I spilled the beans on the dealer, but I was so weird I eventually scared him away. Maybe it was when I told him the metal screen on the door was turning into a huge *vagina dentata*. Or it might have been because I described him aging and becoming decrepit in front of my eyes — using great, grim detail. After he left, giant spiders with glowing red bellies began emerging from the floor, eating me from my feet up, and the flushing toilet in the next room gave me aural hallucinations. I thought I heard my relatives shouting out for help as, one by one, they were being flushed down the toilet due to my betraying them with my fecklessness. I can't remember if that was before or after my liquefied body was sucked up into an enormous hypodermic needle attached to my tailbone. It was the whole fandango, an injured mind declaring war on itself.

The hospital staff never gave me any medication to bring me down, despite my hysteria. They kept me locked in the room until I stopped screaming. I suppose they were operating on the notion that if I suffered more I would be less inclined to take drugs again. As it happens, that was my fiftieth trip (I'd kept count until then). I never fully stopped tripping for six months. They released me the next day because I didn't let on I was still hallucinating. I'd got my first inkling that this drug thing wasn't the great idea I'd thought it was. I didn't do acid again for at least a year.

After I'd escaped from the clutches of the doctors and the university, I spent ten years burning down the road, living hard. I had so much to prove. "The horses which bear me conducted me as far as desire may go . . . ." Parmenides said that more than two thousand years ago, advice I've heeded too often in my career. Then again, every poet wanders a crooked path through literature.

Lugging a big Trapper Nelson packsack made out of canvas and wood, heavy and sturdy enough to pack the hindquarters of a moose out of the bush, I hauled my still-frail body from Mexico to the Queen Charlotte Islands. I adventured, delirious with angst, to Morocco and made it back alive despite the troubles I inserted myself into. I used to hitchhike often to California on a whim. I preferred travelling day and night, in a hallucinatory, sleepless, testosterone-fuelled, bone-aching state, mostly because I had no money, but also because I was desperate to live every moment of the entire day. Relying on the grace of strangers I could reach Los Angeles in 24 hours, though I was still getting picked up by creeps. There were those scary moments of climbing into a stranger's car and spotting the 'rape' door. That's where they remove the window and door handles from the inside of the passenger seat, trapping you until the driver (or someone else) opens your door from the outside. I learned real fast to give the door a hard look before climbing into a car.

It was on the way to California I had to grab a knife off a freeway predator. I took his car keys too, and threw them into the bush before walking off down the freeway, my bleeding thumb out for another ride, while he groped about looking for his keys, complaining — as if I were the bad guy. I had some duct tape in my bag and used that to bandage up my hand. I didn't do a good job, so I was left with a fish-hook-shaped scar on my palm.

My high pain threshold pulled me through more than a few scrapes and accidents. When I broke my leg seven years ago, sliding on some goose shit at a local farm, I reset it myself on the spot, to the astonishment of the old farmer. Then I gathered up the chickens he owed me, and drove off in my ancient, standard-transmission van. When I reached home, I shaved and hand-bathed before going to the hospital. We'd been slaughtering pigs, and I was a filthy, blood-and-fecal-matter-spattered mess. My companion, Sharon, is a nurse, and there was no way I was going to 'her' hospital looking like that. Then the shock wore off, and I nearly fainted from the pain. At least it turned out that I'd set the leg perfectly, and the swelling had locked everything into place so I didn't need any pins. The doctor only had to throw a cast on it, though he recommended I not try setting any broken bones myself again. Shock is a generous physical self-protection. It gives you a window that allows you to reach safety and care. I've learned to appreciate it a few times. Oddly, during the last couple of years, my pain threshold has crashed. I am beginning to think that everyone is given a cup of strength against pain when they are born. I've already used mine up. Now I whimper when I take a good whack. I worry for the future and the pain that still awaits me.

During one of my deranged, hitchhiking runs, returning from Mexico, I caught a ride with a man in a Corvette around midnight in Sacramento. He was a trucker who drove delivery all week in L.A. and wanted to reach his girlfriend's place in Seattle before eight in the morning, because that was when she left for work. He was desperate to get laid, but he was exhausted and needed a driver. The Corvettes in those years were not good touring machines. They were straight-track powerhouses. This car had one of those fruity, miniature steering wheels, so it was hard to control. He gave me the wheel and set me loose on a flat, eight-lane section of the I-5, which allowed me the opportunity to learn how to pilot his high performance toy at high speed. I pushed the car up to 147 m.p.h. (236 k.p.h.) which is the fastest I've ever driven. He would wake up if I slowed below 120. Later, in the early hours of the morning, I struck an invisible bump on the freeway, and the car sailed into the air and came down with a crash, four lanes sideways. We climbed out and checked the damage. I was a little embarrassed because I knew this wasn't my fault. The rear wheel had jumped up when it hit the hidden ridge and shattered the fibreglass fender. The owner glanced at the crack and said: "No big deal. I've done worse. We're losing time." And we were gone again. We made it to Seattle early. He was a real American road-warrior.

This kind of journey became a regular routine.

In the mid-seventies, I was working at a printing shop and I received seventeen days holidays. I decided to visit a friend, the writer Séan Virgo, in St. John's, Newfoundland. By the time I hitched across the country, nine of the seventeen days had elapsed, so I told Séan we had only a single night to party because I had to return home. Séan thought this endlessly amusing. We stayed up all night pub-crawling and shouting poetry at each other until I hit the highway in the morning.

I made it back to Vancouver in plenty of time, despite several outlandish incidents both coming and going, the worst occurring when I was heading east and was picked up by a man driving a brand new candy-apple red van. He was eating speed like it was popcorn (to keep awake) and chugging on a forty-pounder of vodka (to smooth him out). This was a bad, bad combination and he soon went psychotic. He'd also picked up a hippie couple he now decided he didn't like, and he began abusing them. They grew scared and asked to be dropped off in the northern Ontario wilderness. He was too much even for me, so I got out with them. He drove away, but soon returned, racing down the highway, trying to run us over. We had to flee into the bush. A little while later we were picked up by another van, and within a few minutes saw the red van yet again. He almost ran our new driver off the road. By the time we reached Kenora, he'd shown up for another near miss or two, like a red ghost in a horror movie, racing back and forth in the foggy morning. I jumped out at a garage and phoned the police to warn them there was a maniac on the road. Just then he appeared again, and drove straight into a vacationing family's station wagon. Luckily, no one was hurt. He was doing an odd, spastic tarantella in front of his ruined van when the police arrived to restrain him.

On another journey, I got stuck in the wilderness on a lonely highway far north of Prince George. It was a starry night and I was cold, hunched up in my inadequate clothing. I heard something crashing, slow and ponderous, through the bush. My heart was pounding by the time the bull moose thumped its way up over the high gravel shoulder onto the pavement, stopping only a few feet away. I froze, paralzed, terrified. I'll never forget his enormous antlers — up that close it seemed he was carrying the entire night sky in them, all the stars of the universe. We gazed at each other for a moment; then he turned and sauntered across the road and disappeared — just another nice guy going about his business in the dark who, for some reason fathomable only to a bull moose, decided not to charge me. I didn't do much hitchhiking in the dark for a while after that.

I had so much to prove, I tried everything. I was a choker-setter and cat driver, a short-order cook, and finally got to be a clown in a local circus, performing at the Pacific National Exhibition, Playland, and a few local carnivals. I loved my clown outfits. I could be outlandish and invisible at the same time. For a month in Toronto when I was eighteen, I donned roller skates in a book distribution warehouse and would skate like a lonely ghost down the book-laden aisles collecting orders. I was a commercial fisherman, and even a blaster (logging camps actually trusted me with blasting caps, blasting line, forcite, and nitro!). I performed more than a few crazy stunts as a powderman, like playing 'chicken' with other blasters — seeing how many crimps you could put into a blasting cap without setting it off. Miraculously, we retained our fingers. Briefly, I was a film location scout in England and Toronto, but they were pie-in-the-sky projects, and I was totally unreliable anyway. I'd wake up in a logging camp on Haida Gwaii, feeling bush-crazy, and a few days later I'd be in London, on my way to Morocco.

I often got into trouble when I was bunking in that logging camp in the Charlottes — maybe because the islands always felt like my true home, so they unleashed my natural irreverence. Once, a few Haida friends and I snuck up on a black bear fishing in Slatechuck Creek. For some reason we started talking. Our voices scared the hell out of it and the creature shit itself, fleeing into the bush. This gave me the great idea of sneaking up on other bears and scaring them just to watch them freak out. These were only the small, relatively harmless, Haida Gwaii panda-type bears, not the big, mean, spider-legged ones that also dwelt on the islands. This behaviour, repeated only a couple of times, illustrates how crazy and suicidal I was then. Yet I still can't help smiling at the memory of crawling up behind a black bear and going "Booo!!!" Bears sure can jump.

We also lured a 'panda' bear into the cookhouse of a logging camp and fed it canned peaches and ice cream. Now trained, we'd keep it outside, while we waited for a greenhorn, one of the many Toronto *cheechakos* to come in through the regular entrance; then we'd tell him to open the door and let in a little air. The bear would bowl him over on the way to the kitchen. We thought this was droll. Management didn't. The bear got shipped into the woods and we were threatened with termination. Life in the bush.

This was the same company which, after the naive NDP government of '72 announced it was going to protect the rich growth of river-bottoms, immediately cut the giant airplane spruce at Phantom Creek before the law could be decreed. The fallen trees were so large they couldn't be pulled by the steel spars, so they had to be dynamited and the shredded pieces yarded out. Using my height as a measure, I laid myself across one of those stumps three times and still didn't reach the end. That made the tree more than 18 feet across — perhaps the most wasteful use of rare, endangered beauty I ever encountered. I soon escaped the logging multinationals exploiting Haida Gwaii.

I left the Charlottes for the road again. Or maybe I should say I never left the road behind. Later in life, I calculated the highway journeys I could remember, and realized I had hitchhiked over 75,000 miles in ten years.

My sole constant was the pile of manuscript pages I accumulated. I read everything and wrote down my dreams. Still do. I wanted to learn everything. Still do. I wanted to live so hard that I missed most of what normal people would call real life, while all the time I was "half in love with easeful death."

I used to think of my life as the Suicide Express, and when one of the emotional tidal waves rolled over me I'd slash my wrist or step in front of cars or find other spectacular ways of putting myself in physical danger. The reality is that I had no intention of self-destruction, yet I tried to convince myself death was the only cure. Mostly, the cars stopped, though there were a couple of incidents where they didn't. It turned out I had a remarkable ability to bounce. And thanks to the heavy testosterone shots, I healed like a miracle.

I still consider dying every day, but now in a more philosophical than emotional way. The doctor who so casually told me I would not live to forty has long since passed away. My health isn't the greatest, my medical problems exacerbated by the abuses I inflicted on myself, and though I surpassed his prediction more than ten years ago, I'm facing a lot of pain and hospitals yet. With the new developments in medicine, any of 'my kind' slipping into the world will not face as much trauma (or so I'm told), which is good, because there are few horrors worse for a teenage androgyne than being singled out in the showers by the other boys at gym class.

VI

The saddest event of my life took place six years ago. My father died. I was living alone that winter in a cheap hotel in the Yukon, teaching writing workshops and hiding out from the stress that still, on occasion, crushes my chest. Following his funeral on the raincoast I returned to my little winter room, wearing his hat and jacket. I kept dreaming about him — once standing in the snow under my balcony, singing "O Sole Mio" with that impish "here's where we get into trouble" look in his eyes.

After Father was told he was dying, he began sitting for hours, silent, alone in the living room, staring at the TV set. It wasn't on. Who knows what he was seeing written on that blank screen? There are no comforting words for the news of mortality, and I never had the courage to talk to him about it.

Other times he could be ironic. When I was sitting with him shortly after he received the news that the cancer was terminal, he said: "At least now I can eat everything again." He'd grown mighty sick of his 'heart smart' and low cholesterol diet.

Perhaps my greatest inheritance from him was a love of the wilderness. He infected everyone in our family with that love. Father and Mother were on the road from the earliest days, hunting and fishing and just lying about on beaches, or playing cards by Coleman lantern in a snow-shrouded cabin at thirty below until late in the night. I saw a lush nature that no longer exists. The raincoast was one of the great cornucopias of the earth. Biologists tell us that several of the tidal narrows, such as the Burnaby Narrows at Haida Gwaii and in the unique archipelago of the Gulf Islands, once held more species per square metre than any other water in the world. The land was equally rich. My generation ate most of it, and polluted the rest.

Although my parents grew up on the tough streets of Vancouver's East End, both my mother's roots in Grandfather's rural origins and Father's restless spirit took us on the road from the very beginning. The peddling truck was also an escape vehicle, and there was an array of boats over the years. Vague memories from infancy surface often — a small boat hugging the coastline to Squamish because the winding, dangerous highway to Whistler hadn't been built yet. Soon it will be a super highway and Whistler has become a world-famous destination. They were night- blasting the road through then. Every blast would lift our little boat out of the moonlit water, and we'd fall back with a crash onto the mirrored surface. I was terrified. The new Fraser Canyon Highway was also being built during those years. My earliest memories of it consist of stretches of one-lane dirt road overlooking the muddy rapids far below. It took days to reach Kamloops, waiting hours while the blasters cleared away rubble as they punched their tunnels through the canyons above Hell's Gate and other mythical passages.

No matter what desolate campsite or formidable wilderness cabin we ended up in, Mother would have the place organized like a military base in no time, complete with all the luxuries. Shelters were erected, dead rats heaved into the bush, firewood gathered, breakfast and lunch and dinner served as punctually as clockwork. She had a knack for making everything convenient, sometimes hilariously so. We used to drive to White Rock beach when hardly anyone lived there except for summer visitors in a scattering of ramshackle cabins. We camped on the beach and feasted on endless crabs. At Quadra Island, the first one who staggered away from the mighty clam pot was a weakling. For several camping trips to Quadra, Mother decided to travel in style and made Father move the entire bedroom suite into the back of the big peddling truck. You just had to lift up the canvas flap and there was a double bed and dresser. The flap served to protect a full, improvised kitchen on a picnic table.

At a cabin in the Okanagan, I imagined myself menaced by a rattlesnake under our porch. The hot, dry days were bright with yellow lichen and greeny old-man's-beard dangling from scraggly pines. Father would always have curtains of trout hanging on strings; later these would be cooked in butter on cast-iron frying pans while potatoes baked in the fire. Amid the plenty and the gorgeousness, I was fidgeting, always fidgeting — unable to remain still with the world. Sometimes my twitchiness had grim results — like kicking around in the back of Father's skiff while trout fishing, irritated about some ghost only I could recognize in my boredom. Not paying attention to what I was absentmindedly kicking, I booted his expensive new rod-and-reel out of the holder. We both leaned over the side, watching rod, reel, and tackle disappear into the green deep. My father cursed me for hours, "as useless as tits on a bull," he moaned, trolling with a big hook and line for his gear, hoping to snag it. He never did retrieve that rod.

Along with the fishing, he hunted extensively. He shot moose and bears and deer (and an owl once, for target practice — I had trouble forgiving him that one), and hauled them back, powered by his one good leg through a frozen wilderness, armed only with a few smacks of rum and his enormous fortitude, while Mother spent hours canning and preserving and organizing our endless feast. It was a terrific life in the days when we thought the wilderness would never end.

And the wilderness always surprised us, like the day a whale, probably a humpback, surfaced under Father's little boat and skittered him and his fishing partner sideways before temporarily leaving a big hole in the water behind the boat. The year we began fishing Galiano, there were so many salmon we didn't bother with fancy tackle. We used a white rag and a hook. The oyster beds around the islands in the southern reach of Discovery Passage were deep and extensive, often piled so high with nine-inch-long oysters we couldn't beach for fear of punching a hole in the bottom of the wooden boat.

The world was so much bigger and fatter then. My Uncle Arnold, fishing with a boatload of children, including me and my cousins, snagged a ling cod so large that everyone screamed when it surfaced. I thought it was longer than our fourteen-foot dory. Its flattened head was as wide as a Volkswagen Beetle. It looked like a great white shark. Nobody told us the lings got that big. Then it burped up a good-sized rock cod it had swallowed. The smaller codfish had taken our hook and the big ling had swallowed the fish and hook whole. We ate our gift that night with much tall storytelling.

They say that your life is blessed if the killer whale's mist blows over you. If that's the case then I've been blessed several times. It came when my brother was swimming and I was fishing. I remember seeing my lure glinting on the black side of the whale while the mist settled upon us, and my brother scurried up onto the rocks.

The mist arrived when the whales played 'bump the boat' with our dory off Salishan Point. I was a child, staring over the side as the giant jaws opened up a few feet below; then at the last moment, they veered sideways, barely missing us. I was paralyzed with fright. In those days the whales of Georgia Strait enjoyed scaring the piss out of tourists, though they never touched anyone.

The eerie sound of the blow . . . that magic mist . . . it was so haunting and romantic. Yet the truth is they stink dreadfully. Even with my screwed-up sense of smell, the wretched taste in the air of a whale's blow is enough to churn up my cookies just thinking about it. *Amor fati.*

In my teen years we camped for weeks, off and on, during the summer months, at Rebecca Spit on Quadra Island. I used to play fishing games with the eagles. After helping Father clean his catch, I'd tie a salmon head onto my hookless line, and hurl it onto the beach. The bald eagles would swing down and grab the head, my line singing like I had the biggest salmon, and for a brief period I would 'fish' the eagle in the air, as it fought stubbornly for its prize until it snapped the line.

Cleaning the day's carnage out of the boat, I learned how to squeeze the live babies from the bellies of the mud sharks my father hated so much — because they ate the salmon and snagged themselves on our gear — and then I released the babies when he wasn't looking. I would also take the day's offal down to the beach and feed the adult sharks. Their green eyes glowed eerily in the black water; they would leap into the air, fighting over the fish guts, barking a creepy doglike bark, which is why they were also called dogfish.

When I was fifteen and the horror of my condition was upon me, I used to walk the south beach at Quadra, leaping like a twisted-up version of Nureyev from log to log in the monstrous tangles of driftwood that were common then, swinging my radio in time to the psychedelic music just beginning its glory days. I stumbled upon a wounded, starving bald eagle, shot by a bored hunter or irate farmer. Capturing it easily, I took it back to the campsite, where I built a driftwood shelter on the beach, feeding it salmon from yesterday's catch when Father was away fishing, and once, a frozen chicken from the big coolers when Mother wasn't looking. The eagle grew strong, but he never could fly right. My parents became used to his presence, so we took him back home and I kept him in the basement. He was always breaking out of his cage to perch on the freezer (where he knew the goodies were), scaring Mother. I was talked into giving him to the Stanley Park Zoo, because everyone in those naive days believed they could take better care of him. Several officious men arrived, including my bird-keeping neighbour. He tried to grab the eagle while wearing a welder's glove. The eagle drove a talon through both sides of the glove, and the flesh of his hand in the middle. Then the eagle attacked the 'professionals,' and they all fled for cover. I had to gather up the bird for the men. Embracing it, for a moment I stared into those deep, cold eyes, the savage beak only a few inches from my face. During my troubled childhood, I'd somehow learned to communicate with animals by touch, and still can. The eagle knew what was happening, perhaps more than I could admit to myself that day. It was so proud and resigned that I wept as I handed it over to them. Later, I found out they had put the bird down immediately after they returned to the zoo. Never trust authority. They will lie to you, only they don't call it lying, they call it process. When a bureaucrat starts talking to you about 'process,' know that you are going to lose. The means always becomes the end.

Eventually, Mother and Father abandoned the city to live on Vancouver Island, where they grew deeper into each other, their rough wild years becoming gentler, though Father remained dangerous to the end. You never could tell when he would suddenly decide to launch off on some impossible expedition. Only he would know why he wanted to go, and sometimes even he didn't. At the card table, we called him The Knocker, because he often knocked himself out of the games by losing all his money on outrageous bets.

He had a few other nicknames as well. During a childhood escapade he had disappeared for hours. His brothers finally found him hiding stubbornly in the bulrushes. They called him Moses after that. He was always seeking the Promised Land. What was most surprising was that people would feel this insane urge to follow him — perhaps because he was always "looking for a shortcut" — such as the time he got depressed by the funeral for my aunt and, seated in the back seat of my car, directed me out of the graveyard. He hated graveyards: "I'm not dying to get in there." (And he didn't either. We scattered his ashes at Rebecca Spit, where he sleeps with the killer whales and the mud sharks and the salmon.) The shortcut wasn't as easy as it looked, and before we knew it we were facing an illegal u-turn onto a major thoroughfare which we accomplished with my father's many blandishments. The funny part is that the entire funeral procession diverted, following us because they knew I was driving Father and they naturally assumed he knew where he was going, so everyone ended up hooting and beeping and creating an enormous traffic jam on the highway. Moses had done it again. Only he could screw up a shortcut at a funeral. And it seems I inherited his impatience.

Perhaps that's why I must be the only hunter ever shot by a dead duck. It happened on a potato field in Comox, near my parents' home, when I was 24, out duck hunting with Father — I was at the opposite end of the autumn field from Father and my brother, and I was using Father's pump .12 gauge. It had no safety. While watching a fly of ducks, I hooked the barrel on a twig in the blind. Annoyed, I impatiently emptied the bullets onto the ground, but I still blew off my index finger when I flicked away the twig. The beak of a dead duck hanging from the back pocket of my mackinaw must have caught the trigger — and I learned another hard lesson — no gun is ever empty. A bullet had hung up in the chamber. My hand looked like a chicken leg burned over the fire, complete with the white bone sticking out. I searched for the finger, but couldn't find it. Maybe some avenging duck eventually ate it.

Oddly, that was also one of the most beautiful events in my life — it crystallized the world. I will never forget walking across that muddy field. The further half had been planted in corn; it was bright with stubble. I was in shock and felt no pain. I had to hold my hand above my head, otherwise the blood would squirt, and I was pointing at heaven, an image out of a Leonardo da Vinci painting, as I marched across the field. I have never seen the sky so blue, so absolutely pristine; it remains one of the few moments where I felt perfect in a perfect world — until the shock wore off as we reached the hospital. Then it was no fun. Having lost a fair amount of blood, I went white and started dry heaving; the doctor took one look at me and shot me full of Demerol, which gave me a lift — fast. I watched him tune up the bone, clipping it down to a neat roundness; then he sewed the skin back over it. I asked him for a Demerol doggie-bag to take home but he didn't go for that. Those were still the days when you were expected to suffer if sick or injured.

Later, I stayed up half the night playing cards with my family, mostly because my father felt so bad about his gun with its bunged safety. I had to show him the missing finger didn't matter much. I never considered the gun at fault. I was careless. Nevertheless, Father got rid of it. He only used a 'breaking' shotgun after that, and I have that one in my locked gun cabinet now. One day I intend to fill the barrel with molten lead, decommissioning it, and hang it on the wall. Me, I continue to use the pump shotgun that a friend gave me.

My hunting days are coming to an end, like the untainted mountains I climbed and the primeval forests I walked. Tourist highways lead to them now; the forests have been clearcut, the animals endangered, many of the mountains turned into ski resorts or littered with climbing gear. Besides, my knees are ruined. It's winding up for me, and there are other directions to travel. I have killed too much in my life. I love the taste of meat, but the eyes of dying deer haunt me. There are two kinds of hunters — many are surprisingly tender. I know a few who weep when they kill. I've seen others inflated with the kind of cheap pride that comes out of a gun — like those who think money or a flashy car makes them special. These are usually disturbed men, and you learn to avoid them. I've killed dozens of deer in my life, too much livestock, and hundreds of birds, especially chickens. There is something in the eyes of a bird going to slaughter that will stick with you forever — an almost saintlike acceptance.

My first encounter with the sorrow of killing chickens was as a child when my father told me to hold a white rooster over the sink while he cut off its head. The rooster went into the death tremble, scaring me, and I let go. He ran through the house making a gurgly, crowing noise despite the lack of vocal cords, spraying jets of blood up the walls until he ran outside through the front door and finally collapsed, still attempting to crow, on the lawn.

As Donne says, each "death diminishes me," yet at the same time I believe that if you are going to eat meat you should know the guilt of slaying it. I walk around every day with the ghosts of the animals I've butchered. It's a heavy load. I'll probably return in my next life as a racoon, because I've had to kill so many while defending my chickens. I have visions of ascending to heaven in a golden chariot hauled by fifty bloody racoons. Or will I be reincarnated as a chicken? I've slaughtered enough of them. Or perhaps as a deer. Am I looking at myself in the past, or in the future, when I gaze into their dying eyes? Maybe before I die, I'll grow up enough to become a vegetarian, yet I doubt it.

Born into the wild beauty of this raincoast, I can't conceive of living elsewhere, and it was my great luck that my parents introduced me to the festival that nature is — those big black skies full of stars; the glowing northern lights; the phosphorescent effect of the summer ocean shimmering the trail of killer whales beside the night shoreline;

the pervasive whisper of the great September schools of Coho salmon finning, filling a dawn bay with their rustle; the eerie scream of a deer when surprised; or the deer I jumped upon as a thirteen-year-old child, grabbing it around the neck. What was the madness that made me stalk it, barehanded? I trapped it between two sheds at a nearby farm, thinking: *I've got you now*. As if I could contain vibrant life itself. It kicked me in the face so hard I saw stars for hours, and I'll never forget the needle-like drum of its hoofs on my chest as it ran over me.

Who couldn't be possessed by the thousand kinds of moss on the floor of the ancient forests of Haida Gwaii where I saw octopus-rooted cedars thirty feet around, standing in the green luminosity after each rain. The richness of it all — walking along the driftwood beach with my bald eagle friend in my arms, the two of us wounded in our own way, yet trusting each other. He never attacked me once. Richness is barely adequate to describe what we are casually paving, leaving behind only islands of fake, lifeless forests. I miss the grizzly bear that ran over an outhouse and the wolverine that tried to steal my packsack under the midnight constellations. And the fishing line snapping and me leaping into the air on the over-crowded dory while my father cursed and thumped the side of the boat in anger until he realized I had actually snagged the broken line out of the air and was hand-reeling in the enormous ling cod he'd thought we'd lost. I walked through waist-high snow-rainbows in slash-filled valleys and nearly died canoeing over a waterfall because of an insane bet I'd made — that I could run one impossible canyon too many — in flood, naturally.

There was a narrows adjacent to Galiano Island, full of surrealistic life at low tide. As a child, I'd snorkel its length, swimming alongside unafraid codfish, swooshing past anemones, stopping to inspect octopus and wolf eel holes. Fields of bristling sea urchins waved their spines, and the ocean floor adjacent to them was littered with sand dollars. Sea pens and sea cucumbers. Bright sculpins. Abalone. It was a gaudy, undersea treasure house. Today, it is bare and ruined: a desert beneath a multi-million dollar home perched artily on the shoreline.

Being raised out of the rough East End, reaching towards wilderness, gave me the opportunity to know both worlds, along with the many roads my hunger drove me down: the rich, Muslim quarter of X'ian in China; the terrible, damaged prostitutes of Vancouver and the drag queens and drug addicts I used to hang out with in the bad years (no doubt all dead now); the neon dreams of Chinatown; the teeming market in Oaxaca, home of the best hot chocolate in the world, whisked with a *molinillo* by an angelic young woman; the fast cars reaching between cities; a noodle-maker like a Buddhist scholar in Bangkok; the psychedelic revolution of Fourth Avenue and Yorkville and Haight-Ashbury before the drug-use fallout and the Yuppies destroyed those streets.

A friend of mine calls this mess we have made out of our planet 'creative destruction.' I call it a ruined landscape, and I don't have much faith in the human race any more. We sure laid waste to our trail — we may yet evolve into Robinson Jeffers' vision of a destroyed world returning to the simple truths of moon and rock and ocean.

When I turned thirty I realized I was going to die on the road, only I wasn't ready for dying. As with my cup full of pain, I'd used up my cup of luck. I'd heard the warning voice too often. It was neither male nor female. No, that's not true; it was the female voice, the voice of care, even when it spoke with a guttural roar during the first fuelling of my testosterone shots. It would yell at me when danger was coming. It was always right — like the time I was cat-logging on a gyppo show, standing on a muddy hillside near Kitwanga, watching two trapped D-7 cats trying to push themselves out, only they were nudging a key log which, in an invisible chain reaction, released the one above me. I heard my name called deep inside my head. I turned around to see the jagged end of a 40-foot-long log barrelling towards me. Time stopped. The log must have hung up temporarily. I swear I jumped seven feet straight backwards before the log rocketed past, a foot from my nose. The Gitskan Native who was working nearby grinned and said in his laconic Gitskan way: "That was a mighty jump for a white man." When I asked if he'd given a warning shout, he said he hadn't seen the log coming either.

The voices stopped. I was changing. The endless, empty thrills of the road had become boring, and I discovered that the path between the dahlia and the rose in my flower beds was as deep and dangerous as hitchhiking unfinished roads through the jungles of Chiapas in the rainy season, or testing my luck in the Kasbah of Casablanca. The garden path goes deeper, and you have to cultivate your garden. It takes patience, forethought, and generosity — three gifts I'm still seeking.

I met a woman, Sharon, who could tolerate living next to a volcano. I inherited a family, children, and then grandchildren. Each of them is a miracle, like every other living creature. I've a lot of growing up to do yet, and I don't believe I'll have the time to accomplish it. Sometimes I think I've been cheated by having a chemical puberty that's lasted close to thirty years. When I feel ill and sore, I worry that I went straight from childhood to old age without any chance to be an adult in between. My family learned to tolerate (or laugh at) my 'roid' rages and if there's anything I'd want to take back, it would be those emotional outbursts: "There goes Brian again." But that's like telling the horse to stop dying in the bottom field, or trying to heal my street friend thirty years ago — her arms and breasts a wickerwork of scar tissue — from slashing herself every time the world went wrong. And the world is always going wrong.

I assume my almost addictive arguments with the "wrongness of the workings of the world" are what pushed me into politics. And a lot of my interest in politics came from my Italian side, my grandfather especially, although he was never involved in public politics. It was not only his mistreatment and internment during the war, but his sense of fair play and family that inspired me to become involved, whether in ecological, local, national, global, or cultural politics. And now history is repeating itself. The internment camps that housed my grandfather have begun again. All you have to do is substitute Islam for Italian.

In 1980 I made the fatal mistake of writing a long invective against the developers who were ruining the community where I then lived, White Rock. It was published in one of the town's two newspapers.

Much to my surprise (and that of the developers), a few months later I discovered I was an elected alderman. This was bad news for the developers. For a start, I actually read my agendas, which gave me a great advantage over the dinosaurs on council whom I was battling. I calculated I cost about four million a year in 1981 dollars for defeated projects, most of which were ludicrous, or at best, inappropriate, although I was outnumbered seven to one on council. Most politicians are such a self-centred bunch, if you roll a golden apple among them they'll invariably start fighting and posturing. They would vote against projects they supported because I convinced them they would look good doing so. It was hilarious. I was notoriously counter-culture, and survived two elections and four years in office without ever wearing a suit or tie. I've always resented the necktie and have never worn one since the day in high school when a group of 'jock' students grabbed me, stuck my head under a tap to flatten my long hair, and nearly throttled me with a humiliating tie which they forced on me for my graduation photo. I have a deliciously pained expression in that photo. The tie, I regard as a public badge of submission to the dominant business culture of our society — the sign of the hanged man.

I have to admit I did put on a few performances as a politician, most notoriously when I won my second election and showed up at city hall on election night, drunk as a skunk, and enraged. The TV crew filmed me condemning the electorate for their stupidity, although I'd been elected by a landslide. One of the other candidates, elected to the local school board, was a man named Clarence White whose campaign slogan had been "White is Right." He was a former teacher who bragged about working his summer off-months as a gyproc finisher — so he could have a strong right hand for dealing with students who had behavioural problems. That school district, though he is long gone, continues to be accused of intolerance, and recently lost a Supreme Court case for banning books discussing sexual orientation. My appearance that night on TV, two decades ago, standing at a dangerous angle, saturated with brandy, and denouncing the people who elected me, became a legendary political moment in the community.

The local newspaper finally caught up with me in a burst of libellous articles preceding the next election. They even had this guff in the polling stations on Election Day. I went from topping the preliminary polls to losing by 11 votes. I surprised everyone by suing for libel. I don't believe in libel, especially for literary issues, but when it came to manipulating the vote at an election, I felt duty bound. It was a week-long, scary Supreme Court trial. Since they were flagrantly guilty, it turned into a slaughter. I handed over most of my award money to those who supported me during the trial, as I'd agreed before we went to court — including to my lawyer who'd backed me unreservedly and for free during the ordeal — Johnny Blewett, a razor-sharp, shambling man from Saskatchewan, fond of brightly checkered suits and talking like a hick while cleverly outfoxing the opposition's expensive silk-shirted attorney from Vancouver. I bought my parrot, Tuco, with the money left over. For nearly twenty years Tuco has kept me company while I write, diverting me with his arguments about the meaning of life in a crazy universe. The bird understands the absurd and helps me live with the horrors that I read in our newspapers every day.

From my Italian roots I also inherited a love for real food and the garden. According to family lore, Grandmother cooked everything the way she remembered it from Italy. She would spend hours, days, weeks, preserving and stewing and drying and salting while Grandfather tended the vegetables and shovelled the manure. When she died shortly after I was born and Grandfather eventually remarried, our new grandmother, Mary, took up the cooking tradition with equal gusto. The garden was a lush maze from which we could harvest the world, the neat rows of vegetables and fruits meticulously tended. There were raspberries larger than your thumb and tiny, sweet tomatoes. Grandfather knew his meats and he knew his pastas; he was an old-fashioned paterfamilias; you *capisced* what he said — or else! He only had to look at you crossly and your cheeks would start burning. My mother remembers him dragging her around the house by the ear as he touched the counters to check how well she'd dusted them. He pulled my ears a couple of times, too, but I deserved it. The family dinners were full of heated discussions and wine and friendship. Because we were Italian, usually somebody wasn't speaking to someone. Grandfather would seldom engage in these quarrels; instead, he controlled all with a steely eye and the occasional terrifying but quiet reprimand. One of his favourite tricks was to tease with the wine decanter, threatening to withhold it from someone who was too silent at dinner or winning too much at the card tables. He'd wave it around like a benediction from God which, as in real life, could be withdrawn so easily for the most capricious reasons.

For special feasts we'd eat *al fresco*, dozens of us seated at the trestle table, lined up on the patch of lawn behind the house, surrounded by flowers and fruit trees and vines and vegetables. These were the days for the best tablecloth and the 'first' wine from his cellar (he'd only bring out the heavily watered and sugared third pressing when everyone was too drunk to notice), the table overflowing with plenty, Grandmother overseeing the display and the dishes. Nowadays, it would be viewed as a hopelessly sexist affair. It could also be considered a carefully staged theatre, the two actors, Grandfather and Grandmother, effortlessly performing the roles they had cultivated for decades.

Dying of cancer, shrivelled up and tawny-skinned on his bed, Grandfather reminded me of Gandhi. Always a small man, he withered to almost nothing. Yet he retained his dignity and his big heart. When they first put him in the hospital, he took one look at the food, and said, "I'm not eating that crap." So they said: "Okay, we'll feed you by I.V." He said, "Fine, but I'm still not eating that crap." He didn't, either. After several days the hospital gave up. Poor Grandmother Mary had to bring in his meals, or at least enough of them to keep him fed. He probably suffered through the hospital breakfasts. I witnessed one of her charming dinners. He propped himself up, seated nobly in his bed, his napkin tucked into his pyjama top. There was a bowl of minestrone, fresh homemade bread, red peppers in oil, a salad, pasta, home-canned beets, roast chicken, a couple of exquisite little cookies, and a single glass of wine. He finished his meal, patted his lips dry for effect, and as Grandmother reassembled everything into her basket, he pronounced to the other poor, starving patients in his ward: "Now there's a woman that can cook!" He was proud of her and though he wasn't ample with praise, he was free with it when it was deserved.

In his last years I gave him an expensive Scottish scarf for a Christmas gift. I noticed he often wore it on his deathbed at home, because he'd begun to feel cold all the time. I felt strangely gratified seeing him swaddled in that scarf. After he died, the next year at Christmas, I opened my present from Grandmother Mary and discovered the scarf. I started weeping. Everyone received something that had belonged to Grandfather. My parents were outraged at first, especially Mother, because the items were such a poignant reminder. They made everyone cry at Christmas. Yet, after a while, we realized what Grandmother had done. It was perhaps my greatest Christmas present. Thirty-three years later I still have the scarf, and occasionally I feel adult enough to wear it.

My Italian uncles inherited Grandfather's panache, and continued to delight my life. In Grandfather's honour, and as the extended family began to dissipate, I started holding parties to bring us all together. These events came to be known as 'pig parties' because we would roast a whole pig. Everyone was invited. There would be ancient Italian *cumbahs*, local 'shrubbies' (hippie kids who lived in the nearby forest), young poets, old poets, artists, hordes of Italian children, opera singers and farmers, the last of the Cockney fringe from Vancouver, and whomever else we could dig up. These riotous all-night affairs survived everything from bomb threats to divorces. A bunch of punkster kids got caught puffing joints out back by my conservative Italian relatives (with much yelling and haranguing by the elders). There were belly dancers and Scottish pipers who played *Amazing Grace*, accompanying the cooked pig as it circled the house in a primitivist blessing for the farm while the vegetarians fled for cover.

At an early pig party, my two Italian uncles accidentally set the pig on fire while fiddling around with the barbecue. Inside the house at the time, I glimpsed the whoosh of fire from our dining room window.

I raced out onto the deck; there must have been a hundred and fifty people in the backyard. The whole place went silent as my uncles beat out the flames. A lone voice piped up and said: "Oh, oh, here comes Brian." My 'roid' rages were famous by then, since I could go ballistic at the drop of a hat, depending on when I'd last had my testosterone shot. All I could see were purple stars, and all I could think was: *How am I going to feed 150 people a burned pig?* Then another voice, one of my brothers, spoke assuredly from deep in the crowd: "Don't worry; he won't get far with those two." He was right.

My uncles were as cool as cucumbers on ice. By the time I reached the barbecue, they already had the fire out, and had strung some chicken-wire underneath to catch the pieces that fell off. I was so hostile I was spluttering. My Uncle Tony merely said: "You get too excited about these things," while he dusted off the chunks of burnt charcoaled skin, barely able to contain a smile. Then my other uncle, Geno, volunteered: "Sure, Brian, it's not a perfect world." He was a little more restrained because he was the guilty one who'd accidentally started the fire by cleaning up and throwing some butcher's paper under the spit. The pig, naturally, was delicious, as usual, and I still fondly remember the grace of my uncles, Tony now dead, but Geno alive and retaining his aplomb.

There was always a generosity within the Italian side of the family, and they took a shine to my father's flamboyance. By his later years, Father became the open-hearted figurehead around which much evolved. On my parents' fifty-fifth wedding anniversary, everyone chipped in and rented a cabin for them for a few weeks on Quadra Island, where they had summered for thirty years. They were now becoming too old and arthritic for camping. My father's eyes lit up: "Great, now everyone can come!" Though it was a gift for Mother and him, his first thought was to give it back to the family, so we could all go together. The family made his wilderness every time, the way they make mine. It's so difficult to convey his gusto, the loopy ideas that would possess him. He was constantly full of tricks and games. It was like living in a magic show.

There was no stopping Father once he caught a notion. It was mostly fun, but sometimes scary, like the night we had too many beers in the Lorne Hotel in Comox. We'd already beaten everybody at the pool table, and the locals, irritated, decided this old braggart needed to be put in his place. Before I knew it, Father, who was then in his sixties, was arm-wrestling the young loggers and various toughs, crowing: "Come on, I'll take ya'll on." He did, too, wrestling them into submission one at a time, in between a few more beers. The final opponent, a brawny, muscle-bound mechanic, was his match. Father beat him but he strove so hard while slamming the man's arm onto the table that he ripped his own bicep. It sagged down from the bone. The muscle gradually healed, but that was the end of his arm-wrestling victories.

We all learned from him the love of the game, whether it was cards or races. You played everything hard, no matter how foolish it was, and you played it with laughter. Running with the wind was what mattered most, even if you had to run on one leg.

VII

I often think of the word 'weird' in the old Anglo-Saxon manner: *wyrd* — a magical dance of chance and fate, delightful and scary at the same time. Well, it's a weird body and a weird life I was born into, and the words contained within these pages attest to it. This book is my *wyrd* homage to my late father, and my very-alive mother.

He wouldn't have liked all the stories in it, stories I could not have written while he was alive, but we never like all that we receive from the world, do we? He wouldn't have enjoyed the raunchier poems, my harsh yapping at the vagaries of life, or how horribly I behaved out of his sight. There are also incidents he'd think a man should keep to himself. I wish this book could have been closer to his taste. I wish for a lot of things.

Now, Sharon and I run a small, organic, mixed farm. I've abandoned the city of the brutal years, and returned to the rural world I loved in my childhood: those bright, frosty mornings; the lakeside breakfasts; the clank of woodstoves; the radio crackling through the mountains with the early news.

Each day, I learn from the animals how to pay attention. The plants teach me patience. Not enough yet, but I keep trying. It took many years to build up the nerve to tell my story, but I finally realized it was time. Some of this stuff I have never spoken. It yet remains too difficult to speak aloud. I know a few of these incidents will be hard for my family and friends to stomach. They should have tried living it.

When I first began this memoir, I needed surgery and I could only hobble. I was prescribed powerful narcotics to endure the joint pain.

They ruined my guts. It's a great irony that I'm now repelled by variations on the drugs that I embraced for those rough years more than three decades ago. I hated being prescribed morphine. Aside from my stomach, it wore down my body and interfered with my work. A knee replacement has changed that. I still have to take a few painkillers some days, yet I'm back on my feet again, and the decaying joints are keeping me upright so far, though a foot is now crumbling and also needs extensive surgery. But I can go down the road again for a while. I look forward to it.

Though settled down to a degree, the hunger remains. I always loved the Thomas Merton story about the evening he sat alongside the head monk on an idyllic bench in a meadow at his monastery. The ancient monk was quiet as the dark fell upon them. Then a distant train whistle sounded. Despite a lifetime spent examining his relationship with his god in that monastery, the old man suddenly whispered: "Every time I hear that train whistle I just want to go."

The poet, John Keats, said in one of his last letters: "There's nothing stable in the world: uproar's your only music." I can't think of a better epitaph, but only if it includes silence and simplicity alongside the lush and the insane and the noisy. They're all part of the uproar, and I want to know each of them.

Like Tiresias, I've seen glimpses of the female and the male in one body — and the intersex, the middlesex, the hermaphrodite, or whatever you want to call it. They are astonishing. And although I don't believe these glimpses gave me any more wit or intelligence or prophecy, they did give me a varied perspective.

I've been kicked about a fair bit in my life, but I don't hold any grudges. Everywhere I landed I saw a different, exotic landscape — Father's tale of hurling his glowing rivets during the night shifts in the shipyards, Mother making a home out of any wilderness in an afternoon, a Haida friend being dragged underwater in a narrow creek by a giant dog salmon he tried to grab — a fish bigger than him — his friends guffawing as he surfaced a dozen feet downstream. The golden Buddha of Bangkok, and the great Buddha of Leshan near the 1,000-year-old Jade Pavilion overlooking the confluence of the Minjiang, Dadu, and Qingyi rivers. My lost companions from my life on the street. The neon midnights of Chinatown. An underwater statue of the Madonna surrounded by gaudy fish in the Caribbean, and the trees dripping with monarch butterflies on Butterfly Lane in Santa Barbara.

The way I figure it, I'm a lucky creature — it's been a feast. A kaleidoscope. There's a midnight filled with arctic darkness, chasing the aurora borealis through the snow in a jeep, and listening to the electric hum. The Inuit believe the northern lights are the spirit people, the dead, playing a game of soccer. Many times I've considered joining them. It must be an elegant game up there, to be dead yet rustling through those shivering curtains of colour. And I've also had the opportunity to haul a living lamb out of the slit-open belly of its dead mother, to heap black earth around the bright green of spring's first fava beans, to bury my old dog finally dead after years of her unfailing love, and then raise a lucky puppy that refused to drown in an icy pond. Bitter moments can't be denied, the nights crying into my whisky — until I go to bed and it starts again. Every warm-hearted dawn impresses me, every day is an adventure and an absurdity, and then the gaudy sunset leads to the magic that arrives with the night.

Interlude

Only after I'd assembled *Where We Live* did I understand that it was an homage to my genetic history and my family — my late father, and my very living mother. Father and I didn't always have a smooth relationship. While this is true with many sons and fathers, we were a spectacular pairing. Out of our history, and the whirlwind of my younger years, came the world of these poems.

There are more than a few incidents here that my mother found repugnant, but I'm proud of her acceptance of my reality and her permission to publish this. I'm grateful for her forgiveness for my telling some of these awkward stories from the past, and for her understanding of my need for blind honesty. I hope the rest of my family will be able to react with the same generosity.

And being the child of a storyteller, I must admit I don't al-ways let the facts get in the way. Although most of these poems are based on experience, they often changed in the telling, revealing their truth in details that are not always autobiographical. I guess I have developed that ability, common to those who have been hurt, of seeing into the mind of the other — the tendency to analyse the madness that caused the hurt. I have also used incidents that happened to me, but grafted them onto created characters because the characters I create in fiction have a different truth from that of the ones I meet in real life, and honesty to a story is more important than mere imitation of a person. Most writers do as I have done.

A memoir, of course, is a different kind of story, and here, I have followed my memories, those of my mother, and whatever facts I could dig up, as accurately as possible. I like to think of the memoir and the poems as mirror images of each other: the same well, but viewed from within and without.

So it's public now. That is the story and these are the poems.

Salt Spring Island, 2004

Where We Live

I

WHERE WE LIVE
for Chris and Roben

With mud wattles and caves or wood,
    on stilts in water, near water,
or facing water (best glittering)—we build them.
    There are homes
    where the tender sounds of sleep
give comfort to babies and cats on chairs.
Children, I sent you out, watched you shut
the door behind your back, making your moves,
making your own homes, walls, gardens—
    sitting under trees in the grass,
    watching your own children
    dream of life that resembles water,
    the water in basins, water running
or stagnant in damp ceramic jars next to the fire.
    Because every house also needs a fever,
the crack of cedar kindling, oak roaring against the night,
    and someone to sit alongside within walls—
gazing through glass doors or casements or battle windows.
Steel, stucco, adobe, palm leaf, stone, wood, cement, even snow;
    we live everywhere
and use everything, pulling it over our heads
    like bugs in the Amazon.

Some are born under broken roofs, some are starved out,
    evicted, bombed, evacuated.
Oceans will take them away, lakes, and volcanoes.
But an urgent desire in the flesh makes the legs
    come back.
It makes the meat of many human arms work together

to lift the mighty roof beam.
It is the hunger of our evolution, the *eikos*
which demands shelter and protection and sleep.
   It is the history of families singing,
a question that needs no answers, only affirmations—
   all of us want to go home.

THE SWIMMING HOLE

I'm sorry,
    my darling
but the chores are undone,
    the lambs unfed,
    the wood unchopped,
    the beans not weeded.

It was hot
    and the sun lives
in a strange sky.

It made me think of many things.

    I found myself at the lake,
    floating past the dock,
where girls with enormous breasts
sun naked on the cedar planks
while the skinny boys pretend
they are only dancing in water,

but I was not watching.

The sky unnaturally blue,
    the bullfrogs humming among the lily pads,
I was drifting in a black lake,
    stunned by a single scudding cloud.

It's the swimming hole.
What can I say?

There are so few of them left.

I floated away
on my back, defenceless
in a changing world,
the limpid water
very soft,
and very sweet.

THE FROG ON THE GATE LATCH

More brilliant than an emerald on wood,
the tree frog sat out the morning, taking its sun
the way some of us take our wages—
demanding only what we deserve and nothing more.

In the golden burn of the afternoon
it found the shade the latch provided.
Later in the evening, when I watered the orchard
and fed the sheep, I noticed it again,
still perched on that strap of cedar
which barred one world from another—
imperious, like a bright emperor, its hooded eye
studying me for false or dangerous moves.

There were none in my heart, not this night,
and I slid the latch home with a tenderness
the brittle wood hadn't known for some time—
    the gate an ancient victim
of the aimless battering of sheep, the escapes
a horse devises with its rubbery lips, or my despair
after a hard day making nothing out of stupid dirt.

This small green king offered grace and patience
while requesting only a perch for itself.
The gates might open and shut and we may
often find ourselves lost in our own homes,
    but there is always someone else,
    ready to embrace our crazy landscapes.

THE BODY OF YOUR ATLAS

The tongue is a weapon made for love,
delicate and wet and dangerous.
We use it to create far-fetched and ironic
tales about the body and maps of flesh.
I brushed it across her lip, and she murmured
all the old stories, making them new again.
She laughed like an uncensored romantic.
Take me into dark places, the meadows of night
where the wind whispers in the seared grass.
I touched her eyelid, that tender shield
but all I could find was her question.
What does it mean when I greet you with my eyes shut?
Then the swelling lobes of her ear, and inside,
        deeper, sealing out sound.
I can hear you when you mouth my silence.
        She wanted the eternal game.
We discovered the neck, the elegant isthmus
joining continent and island, such smooth sand,
the tides of pale desire awash like seashells.
Into the gap we fell, that voluptuous hollow
where the collarbones meet, and further,
        until she whispered:
That was such an epic journey.
Ah, your fake mountains, the little cordillera
capped with glaciers of black ice,
that melted snow, those naked peaks.
        Then you laugh again,
because you are embarrassed and hungry
and your laughter is almost a sensual weeping.

This story is the endless story.
Ripe metaphors repeated over and over again.
As if you know the dementia that strikes
those who trek the adventure of skin and desire
where geography becomes love
    in an extended joke,
and love goes an unknown distance.

DOMESTIC NIGHTS

The cold comes clean at last,
sharp and biting from the north,
a snap in the air and hoarfrost on the earth.
The world turns to crystal.

It's late, and the Dog Star
is almost red above the horizon.
We walk down the rutted road,
cracking ice on the puddles
for the black dog's delight.

Beneath the hazy river of the Milky Way,
in the crackle and stillness of winter
I discover myself smiling at this darkness.

We are never what we think we are.
I always thought I'd die on my road,
alone, running from those demons
that caught me on the day I was born.
But after two decades together,
all the fights and threats and laughter
and armageddon dreams, we are still walking,
    with smiles on our faces,
towards midnight under the almost permanent stars.

IN THE MINDANAO DEEP

In the Mindanao Deep
there are fish designed
to hunt prey larger than themselves.

They snatch their victims
by the belly, break them
in two, fold them over
and swallow them whole.
This reminds me of my first wife.

But I wouldn't wish her cruel
returns for all her adventures,
not leeches on her body,
or chemotherapy hair,
nothing as wild and ugly as that.
No, I offer her my good love,
and good hunting too, swimming
down there in her dark waters.

A VERY CANADIAN DIVORCE MOMENT

There was that female glance of yours—
the too-early annoyance in the morning.
    It told everything,
    as I turned towards
    the streaks of dawn,
and saw our red canoe, left untied again,
drifting far away, empty, on the blue lake.

FALSE SUNRISE AT FIFTY-TWO

So it was a night of fights, and I'm going
to be, or not be, divorced again,
although we never got around to getting married.

This has almost become boring.

And only last week I was explaining to a friend
the nuances of twenty years of domestic life—
how some of us never fight for the first ten years,
and then make up for it over the next ten,
until we just give up and get along.

Love always has its surprises. I like them.

I slept in the spare bedroom
with the cat and a bottle of whisky.
At three a.m. even the cat abandoned me.
Finally, I arose and awaited another
year of sunrises, drinking more whisky
and sweet tea with milk. It was luxury.
The mist above the ponds. She was sleeping softly
upstairs, alone, wearing only the grief we'd constructed
over decades of mystery and laughter and anger.
I wanted to rejoin her, but knew I could be
            knifed in my sleep.
So I waited and I drank, and for some reason
got all excited about crêpes suzette with sugar.

When you're fifty-two, the thrills
may come from strange places.

You can also find them in those false sunrises
that promise a light show of mist and colour
but deliver only the sun.

BREAKFASTS FOREVER

After fifty daybreaking years,
I still wake up hungry;
    perhaps
it's the murderous promise of a false dawn
or the shadow-memory of yesterday's frenzy—
    but there's a lion in the belly.

He's been sleeping and feeding for years,
yawning expansively after sex and cigarettes.

Twitchy antelopes crap themselves
    when they see my teeth.

Hey, I'm awake and I'm hungry.
And it's not for a lack of feasting—
I've already eaten the pig and the leaf and the garlic
and the crocodile caught in the swamp.

    I wake up raging with delight,
smiling voraciously at songbirds, rubbing my hand
on the sleek, oiled mahogany chair
beside the bed, while floating in my
nest of goose-down and sunshine.

    Good morning means just that.
The world is everywhere. It tells me
the history of desire, in my eyes, in my skin,
    my mouth
when I taste the smell the dew makes on the grass.

But the scent of you is all over me now,
    like the memory of my tongue
sliding up one side of you and down the other.
    Yes, you were
    breakfast before breakfast,
luxury accompanied by the haunting call of the thrush
who signifies everything that's real in a west coast dawn.

The bird whose song is the signal that starts another day
    in the life of striving, the life
    we live whether we want it or not—
    like work, a word made ugly
    by a culture fearing sweat and heat,
    sticky skin, and broken fingernails,
    although work is what we do.

    Work is the oily gloss
shimmering the clay on the wheel.
It built Karnak and sphinxes—
all the shadows and creations
    and archaic stories;
work is when we walk with
and learn from the orangutan
while returning it to the jungles of Borneo.

Our labour hums oddly in the heart
of the office, bringing
    everyone together—
bad bosses who need enlightenment
standing next to water-cooler heroes.
    It carves the sacred
blue scarab from shivered marble.
    Work is women and men

collecting rubber, collecting garbage,
catching fish, sharpening knives,
writing algorithms and stuffing them
into the back of a book where they
    will never be seen again.
It's the polite and the cranky and the ignorant
    answering questions,
        or
    not answering questions.

    Work is a poem dancing
    like a water strider
on the surface tension of the world.

Did Shakespeare know he was Shakespeare,
or did he only know the work to be done?

    Work is how we live,
    trying and failing,
    and returning again,
creatures a-glisten in the sheen
of aching muscles and stressed-out sighs,
and then getting up and trying once more,
    beyond even the idea of again,
like these birds in this ghostly dawn,
    the time of our greatest hunger.

    Breaking the fast?
There wasn't one to begin with.
    I've been feeding since
    the day I was born;
now I'm going to feed some more.

Consider the egg:
wonderful and white,
    or brown,
    or blue,
    or speckled.
I've spit out their shells everywhere,
in Morocco and Glasgow and Mexico.

Miracles of life and mornings—
    like the Beijing breakfast
    begun with the brown,
    husk-coloured ring of cold rice
    remaining in the old iron pot,
warmed with hot water and tamari sauce, and
served with pickled vegetables and fried dough,
    chased by a hot broth of millet
sipped from a mutton-fat-glazed bowl.

    Crêpes rolled in sugar,
and steamy croissants washed down with black
espresso in a cup as small as a mink's skull;
    watermelons and strawberries;
sweet, sweet oranges; carved cantaloupes
    on a plate, with cream.
Fat raisins studding a toasted seed bread.

Cereals: oats and rye flakes and flax,
pumpkin and sunflower seeds,
cracked wheat and the good bran
surrounding every organic shell—
that's what goes into this boy's
    bowl of morning mush.

There was the young mother in the market at Oaxaca,
bent forward, almost offering her breasts while
ladling creamy hot cocoa into a cracked mug
lovingly made from local earth by a local potter.

There were ham and eggs fried with tomatoes
accompanying re-cooked black beans and shredded
    potatoes sizzled on a grill.

French toast with sugar dust and maple syrup
and butter oozing over the grids on the waffle,
and then more syrup drowning slabs of pancakes.

    The great, bitter heart
of the grapefruit I picked, leaning
from the deck of a cabin in Costa Rica.

I don't want everything,
    only a little taste,
the honey in the muffin,
the salt on the loaf of your thigh.

And no, I will never forget other brown sugar lovers
or that erotic butter melting like ice on a griddle,
    while the rush of the world skates
across my ancient menus, these twice-served memories of feasts,
    our history and the old stories,
    all arriving with this mahogany reflection
    of light falling on the slickness of your thigh
    amid a torrent of bird songs.

    Best of all, once
we have finished our breakfast—
    then, we can go to work.

THE TEARS OF THE PREDATOR
(Rumour, probably apocryphal, tells us that James II of England, a great gourmand, was once so impressed by a beef roast that he hauled out his sword and whacked the tasty dish, knighting it: "sir loin of beef".)

The history of the world is, my sweet,
the story of who gets eaten and who gets to eat.

—attributed to Sweeney Todd

Does the lion weep for the zebra,
    the otter for the crab,
        the starfish for the clam,
the ape for the mound of grubs in its paw,
    the wolf for the mouse?

    Does the raven weep
for the pierced breast of the starling,
the crow for the fat walnut cracked on a highway,
the slippery mink for the eleven chickens
    with their throats ripped open—
wandering across the forest floor like zombies from a bad film,
as silence follows the last ebbing streaks of blood and life?

Does the cougar lament the deer,
and does the lettuce scream
its terror at the cutworm—
    or worse,
shriek at the teeth of the gourmand
    penetrating a light vinaigrette
    before ripping cellular matter?

A scream made more terrifying
by the knowledge that only
another lettuce leaf could
    hear or understand it.

I don't know who weeps for what,
or if anything cries real tears,
but I've thought about the salmon
splattering blood in my boat,
the many potatoes
    I innocently tortured
    over a campfire,
the roast of venison simmered
with garlic under a cowl of fatback.

I know personally
    the rooster that I hung
        to bleed from the evergreen
for a little stew to start in the morning after its last day.

    I pack the lives of the dead
    in the suitcase of my stomach.
    their histories and their hopes,
    and sometimes I even weep when I eat.
    But I celebrate the luxury of every meal,
and sing at the table the hungry song of good wine,
the carved, the spiced, and their verdant companions.

SUIMONO SOUP IN AN ORIBE BOWL
a recipe for Graeme

A delicate *dashi* broth—
simmer briefly
shaved tuna flakes,
a chunk of *kombu* seaweed;
    then strain.

Garnish with a sliced
    bamboo shoot,
the knife-thin slivers
from a green onion,
    and reverence,
which makes all food
    taste like art.

THIRTY YEARS BEYOND MIDNIGHT

After midnight the fire blazed
beside the pond, reflecting
the moon-tinted water lilies.
We were shadows perched on rocks,
tending our oysters steaming in their shells,
slathering them with butter, garlic, herbs.

The feast, good friends, drink, laughter;
unlike the body, the memory never ages.

FALL DOWN
for Ajra

I love the way little children fall,
their almost graceful clumsiness, snatching
from a race for a toy, a two-footed fall.
Then the knock, the bounce, and the moment
when she looks up, astonished, studying
everyone nearby for witnesses,
as she recognizes she is hurt—
the wide-eyed open-mouthed
pause that precedes a yell, the shout
against the awful indignity of pain
until she wanders off again, distracted
by the next event in a day full of wonders,
having taught us how elastic the world is.

BRANDED

The men around here are branded
    by the land,
notified of history by their skin,
    livid on a blustery day.
    My veneer is an entrance
for all my wounds, all my memories.
    I only have to look at my body
and a cowbell rings in the woods like those
dreams of pain I almost forgot long ago.
O my skin is dying. Pale slivers
    crawl across the flesh,
    emaciated incidents
that became metaphors for the past.
Here is where the lamb bolted when
I clamped the bedessars
onto its testicles and we both
    ended up screaming.
There is the joke of the fence—
three fingers caught in the sudden gate.
    These scarred knuckles remember
    the letterpress that printed my blood
    all over someone else's literature.

This living, it hurts; we strive
against the wind, against the land,
against the plastic reality of our time.
And we make small wounds in our surfaces,
the first one oozing—the second one cauterized—
the third one a permanent reminder.
    Each day
I wake up in the morning and I am healing everywhere.

II

DROUGHT

Do you know the taste of dust in your mouth?
The ash of dry dawns?
The sun a red thumb pressed against the horizon?
Do you know the tragedy of cattle on their knees,
the board shrinking away from the nail,
the motor dead with gravel in the oil?
A world of unwashed clothing and caked dishware?
No showers, dirty vegetables, the pipes banging?
The filthy child spotted with sores?
Do you know honest, brutal drought,
the kind that parches the spirit while far away
the vaguely concerned cluck into their Perrier
at Alberto's coffeehouse beside the ocean?
Do you know the endless dust of each day,
the fuel for black fires, and the black mud
at the bottom of the pond when all the water is gone?
Every skyline foamed with the clouds that avoided you?
It's the old story of hope and desire,
the kind that makes you a voyeur of lost storms.
It's a world of waiting and yearning, the crazy knowledge
that even this desert must someday inherit a green rain.

CONSIDERATIONS OF ANARCHY

The old poet and writer of fiction—
that's him in the photograph beside the door,
the little fellow with the moustache,
the aesthete with a taste for whips
    for women in leather,
the man with a trembly upper lip
which made him resemble a rabbit
    when he ate his lettuce—
once said to me, years ago:
Everyone should be an anarchist
at the age of twenty.

This was the knowledge of a man
who had gone beyond sixty years,
and had come to love the conservative,
    who raced his horses
    and drank the best cognacs,
who denied what he used to believe,
concluding that all of us will
eventually Judas the life we once lived.

Young then, I thought it wise of him
to understand the boil and tidal ebb of blood,
the hormones that control the run, the rush....
But today, when I contemplate not just
my own unfinished home and garden,
but the gardens of those who can afford gardeners—
I can only witness the savage landscape
we have made out of our collapsing planet.
Perhaps this is why, now that I have
more than doubled my years, sometimes,
I want to burn down all our houses.

NO ONE MOURNS THE COOK

A man falls in the morning
and no one recognizes him.

    It's religion.
    It's faith.
    It's hope.
    It's a delusion of the heart.
    Maybe it wasn't him.
    "Maybe they're just birds, honey."

A man dies in the morning
and a chorus of fools screams:
    "Never forget!"
because they have already forgotten
those who fell in the mornings
    of every century.

A man dies. A woman dies. A building dies.
    thousands die—
including a few pigeons
    and tapeworms.
But no one mourns the cook.

He is an illusion in a photograph, suspended
in perfect lines, resolute, diminishing—
    the falling man.

Great figures of history swagger onto the stage
and make power points, quote satisfying words
written by the hired makers of memory.
    That's their job,
and nobody mourns the anonymity of the flaks.

History remembers the proud mayor in the ruins.
It remembers the defiant words of a president
who'd spent the day hiding on an airplane.
    But it doesn't mourn a man
    who might have been a cook.

And I want to remember the cook,
    like I want to remember
the tiger chasing the sauce maker
who was merely looking for a mango;
the chuckwagon full of beans
    driving over a cliff,
    porcupined with arrows.
    No one mourns the cook.

    He's good for a laugh,
    or he couldn't die that way,
    or he was a secret hero wearing an apron.
    And so we begin the denials.
    He was a good man.
Good men don't swan for 107 storeys.
And they aren't caught by a camera in a moment
    of impeccable fortitude
before they are stripped naked by the wind
and shatter like the embarrassing fragments of a life.
    That was someone else.

Are only the beautiful woman and the beautiful man
praised by artificially constructed memories
    that insist death has symmetry?

A man plummets from the towers
in what might be a pressed white serving jacket—
    upside down, one knee bent
head pointed to the earth far below.

Who remembers the cook on the *Titanic*,
the ugly gunsmith at Rourke's Drift
and the table arranger whose napkins
    rose up like angels
    when the bomb went off,
the fat woman jouncing down the burning road,
    unfortunate gravity
making a caricature of a life fully lived—
the innocent lovers perfectly smashed by the surprise
    called the foot of Godzilla?

Earth, take them:
    the happy fast-fry lady,
    the soup maker from Salvador,
    the uncomplaining gravedigger,
    the old logger, the master, who saw the trunk
    of the great Sitka spruce turn around
    and splatter him when it fell the wrong way.

They are dying every day,
lonely in their imperfection—
these people of this world.

And no one mourns the cook.

Earth take them,
and deliver their ashes
home.

They have been mutilated, cast off,
drowned, maggoted, vaporized, cancered,
raped to death and dumped into a well.
Earth, take them.

The cook and the tailor
and the nurse who wears glasses,
the big-breasted blonde running the forklift,
the men walking into walls watching her.

They just wanted a job
and they were given a bag
full of bombs when they drove through Basra.

"We have faith."
"I have faith."
"The fire will go around me."
"Go around me, fire."
"My god tells me I will survive."

Then the walls came down,
and the towers fell, and you could hear the roar
all the way to Baghdad. You could hear it in Kandahar
when the helicopters dropped their revenging angels of fire
on the wedding party.

And now no one mourns the cook
because we don't know who he is.

He could have been Norberto.
He could have been Jonathan.
He could have been Joe or Mike
     or even a secret Alice.
Instead, he is only an image in a photograph.

     The names mean nothing.
     The living creature is everything.

This is the falling man of your history.
     And now you will forget him,
the way history has forgotten millions of other lives.

THE SOLDIERS OF AL-QAEDA

Who of the scrub hills is among them,
    who from Kabul and who from Kandahar,
who late of the fig market, or the tire salesman
who abandoned his children and his young wife,
who never saw his grandfather in his deathbed,
    who vowed to die and then lived;
who was displayed on his knees in a Cuban prison,
who has a white towel draped over the back of his skull,
who had his beard shaven; who saw the light;
who could have raced camels for a living, but
    who rode a tank;
who blew up children and cut the legs off a man
    who sang on a public street;
who might have been a shopkeeper in the wrong place;
who didn't like invaders, or
    who was a foreigner
        who walked in rags or riches,
            who carried a rocket launcher;
who are they, the soldiers of Al-Qaeda
    who are kept in cages,
        who could be victims or innocents,
who might be patriots or enemy combatants or terrorists,
    who are not prisoners of war,
who know this because that is what they're told by the soldiers
    who captured them;
who could be caged many years for the crime of our not knowing
    who they are, or
        who they killed, or
            who they didn't kill, or
        who might not even be soldiers;

who could be politicians
who use cant and fine phrases, and imprison those
who have a different skin or a different nation;
   who might hurl millions into an unholy war;
who are the terrifying soldiers of Al-Qaeda?

AWKWARD TRAVELLER

The voices are so distant,
is it just cheap receivers?

Every call from a strange place.

    I've left the Yukon River,
and I'll contact you again when I am in Faro.

    Or the more extreme
notes from landscapes beyond
    the reach of the telephone.

    It's wild in Chengdu,
but I know where the garden is now,
        and yesterday I saw fire orchids.

Then the return, the assured yet tentative greeting.
    A touch on the cheek.
        Yes, it was a good journey.

    To think this is the woman
he penetrated five times in one night
    of sweat and whisky,
        crushing each other so hard
the stink of love was etched permanently into the sheets.

He threw his luggage into the trunk and she drove back
up the hill of a thousand rides.
    Has it been twenty years together, already?

How time catches us,
lunging faster as we slow,
our bodies filling with lead.

Later,
    when she was asleep next to him,
    saturated with the deep
    night of the forest surrounding the house,
    her skin almost feathery,
he remembered the owl guarding the tree beyond the window,
perhaps beause she was also breathing like a bird,
    bird and woman—
a tender sound that made him wonder
    if that's what he would hear when
the tiny blood vessel broke inside his brain.
Near motionless, she was
       a sleeping bird god,
    always dangerous,
and he wondered:
    How will I ever find you again?

    When was the year their history
    turned her heart towards stone—
    he couldn't remember it.
    But he was quiet and careful,
sidling up to her and sliding alongside
    her naked shoulder, slipping
    his little finger into her palm,
    knowing that her hand would
    close upon it the way a baby,
    once you touch its palm,

will always enclose you.
The gentle pressure made him smile,
and his thoughts, for a moment, were
all mixed up
with birds and gods and history and women.

NORTH OF YICHANG

Two ships pass slowly under the moon
shining on the Yangtse River,
beyond the great gorges.

    Going home,
my thoughts are on you.
A stranger visiting the old kingdom
I watch the illuminated windows,
of the passenger ship—searching
for life in this humid night,
but I see nothing—no glorious,
unguarded moments, no hot bodies exposed,
only strangers gazing back at me,
    as if there are
    no lovers in China,
or am I just looking at the wrong
    side of the boat?

THE TOURISTS ASCEND DRAGON GATE PASS

Poling up the gorge,
the old bargeman leaning into
his spiked bamboo rod
knows all the ancient ballads.
Ho, divine river.
Ho, hear my song.
Ho, hear it again,
for I am old and worship your water.

The passengers are bored.
They've already bought enough trinkets,
and the river is long.

A gaunt boy who lives in the hovel
gouged into the mountain,
runs along the riverbank
as the tourists from Chongqing amuse themselves—
throw Yuan notes into the torrent,
watching them float past the little boy
too scared to dive into the river, but following
like a sandpiper on the shore,
the course of lost
money in the emerald rapids.

THE GO PLAYERS OF BEIJING

Just when we think we have nothing
we have a birth day in Beijing.

The ordinary becomes mysterious when it's your birthday—
your own holy quest—finally seated at a raggy table
in Chenwanmen, waiting for the Beijing Duck.

Bring on the enchanted pancakes,
the bitter plum sauce from heaven!

Like the ancient puzzle
carved from the tusk
of the burnt corpse of an elephant
you receive mysteries inside mysteries.

Here, on another endless street, alone in Beijing,
you will find the magic of murder and wonder.
Now stop, look at where you have wandered, look—
this road is your gift.

A street of Mongolian fur traders
sideburned and bewhiskered,
deliciously arrogant and draped
with furs in the afternoon.
They ignore the equally pompous Russian
dignitaries scrounging for luxury—
bureaucrats whose love of exotic pelts hung
like casual treasure
is worth little attention,
as the men from the desert glare at their painted boards,
captured, like you,
playing the game of Go for a lifetime.

THE MASTER CALLIGRAPHER'S SCHOOL OF X'IAN

After dusk I left the Muslim quarter,
alleyways of truth in living—passionate and narrow,
    where bored men brace the walls with their backs.
Their breath filled with shouted questions from doorways,
    and all doors use a strange language, for a stranger.
I am going nowhere and embracing confusion faster.
    The shadows in the winding lanes made a locust sound,
made silence surround the clack of footsteps.
    I'm out of one ghetto and into another, between
vats of small red peppers and the brushmakers.
    Dried bats on a table and plastic ladles,
the evening sky full of laundry like surrendering flags.
    I'm lost. I've been lost for years.
No direction but everywhere. Is everywhere a direction?
    A man appears at my side, flashing small teeth
and a big grin. He takes my sleeve, offering the hope
    of pigeons flying home to the temple.
Suddenly, it's cool, shady, and narrow.
    Ceramic lion-gods defend the corridors.
Now I am totally lost, and I know he could kill me.
    And I think if I die, well, I die.
Then I find myself in a room, a scholar's sanctuary
    so silent in the enormous city
it could be a grassy valley beneath blue
    razor peaks, a lost dream kingdom,
mysterious within the ancient capital of X'ian.
    The walls are covered with leaping horses.
Green dragons, blue waterfalls, yellow carp.
    Facing a table as wide as ten coffins, he touches
my hand with his, and unrolls beauty from terror.
    Back out in the street I cradle a scroll,

brush-stroked in the aristocratic style of the ancients,
    paid for with unmurdered gratitude.
It's a poem by the master—Li Po—
    who died falling into the river of life.
They say the moon's invitation took him, a fever
    in a reflection, like the passions of today,
the fever of the city spawning people in a labyrinth,
    the eagerness of absolute existence,
the yellow moon shining above the dark streets of X'ian.

X'ian, China, May 2000

PANIC ATTACK

Waking up, startled, at sooty midnight,
I can't breathe, sucking air, but it isn't enough,
it's never enough, and suddenly I know
I'm going to die soon. We're all going to die,
you children, you friends, you lover—we're
all sinking into the greasy muck. My mind was
racing through the jungle, past the empty
cobra hole, the skinny pink leeches reaching
from palms and vines as I stumbled across
the trail of the wild elephants—their reek
permeating the debris, the trampled bamboo.
I stood among the water-pooled
footprints in the swamp at Kao Sok,
that last refuge of tigers and Java rhinos.
The weight is crushing my chest again.
Am I dying? Or have I only been
stepped on by the dreams of elephants?
North, in the gardens beyond Chiang Mai,
the beasts labour, grey ears bleeding scarlet
from the iron hooks of the *mahouts*
as they prod them down the trails—
hauling endless tourists for bananas.
The fake 'hill-tribe' women murmur,
perched on their rickety, bamboo stands,
pleading for someone to buy a trinket
while I look away, towards something lost
behind the huge, wise eye of the elephant.
Then I am twisting in the sheets again,
gasping for breath, the enormous rush
of death's promise riding the elephants
through the jungle in a dark rain gaining speed.

LADY MORPHINE'S NIGHTMARE HOUR

She takes your hand,
  leads you with her soft energy,
the burning eyes lined by the shadows of sleep,
Morpheus, the man/woman god,
    changing colour and shape
    to match your desire.
Lady Morphine, she comes sliding over me.
    It's not the first sleep
    but the second sleep
    that kills your dreams.
Ghostly hands trickle up your thighs,
    massaging your temples—
    a tongue licks your itchy skin.

Lady Morphine
wears a different face every morning.
She keeps them in liquid-filled jars.
She offers perfect love at dawn, when
the sun shines golden on her green skin.

Lady Morphine
I love every one of your faces,
I love your sick children, too,
    all your twisted relatives,
deformed and inbred, born in
the back hills of the laboratories:
heroin, leritine, dilaudid, codeine, demerol....

Opium-deceiver-whore-mother-companion,
    the world made easy with a needle.
    until you shatter us into fragments,

unleash your monsters, your bad brothers,
mottled octopi sliding across ocean rocks,
screaming Rottweilers with mouths
    larger than open mine pits—
assassins and rapists and muggers and tarantulas.

    Lady Morphine
    takes your hand;
    she takes your love,
    and then she takes your life.

THE HONEY GUIDE

The girls are working their wings like smoke in the petals,
creating the hum of the afternoon, fetid with heat,

I go looking for a honeyed thing.

Gold is not an emotion.
     Gold is an intellectual construction. Surfacing
in the seventh layer of Schliemann's digging
     through the tombs of the empires.

In the wide fields of my youth I saw red gold—
even tasted it; now it's liquid with memory,
like the years chasing crayfish in the shallows.

     There's a noise surrounding me,
these wings, this language of scent and motion.
     Imagine—living off flowers!
The honeybee knows all talk and direction
     is a dance, scented and sung.
I will fly three hundred miles every day.
I will be perfectly guided by an unknown force.
I will dance my entry to the womb each return.
I will die in the shudder of many wings.

But in Africa there's a bird wounded with intelligence,
     the honey guide.
It fake-breaks its wing on the ground and limps
     crippled towards the hive,

luring apes or hungry people—to make havoc.
Now close your eyes and imagine the mind of that bird.

>*I am the lord among thieves.*
>*I will take you to the zone where the queen hides.*
>   *And when you steal your fill,*
>   *(a theft like smoke)*
>*I will eat the remains, and be satisfied,*
>   *I am the honey guide.*
>*I live on the sweet ruin everyone leaves behind.*

PRAISE FOR THE CHEAP HOTEL

I have this friend
who travels with her own pillow.

She'd heard the stories
of dust mites and detritis
and the human ash left behind
as we burn our own skin just being alive,
how a black light will reveal the stains
that remain from love affairs and porno films.
        I know another man
who won't turn a tap off in a public washroom
for fear of contaminating what he's just cleaned.

Well, I've slept in the dirty sheets of others,
        laid myself down
                in the dust of my ancestors,
slept with relatives unmet.

You can't embrace beauty
until you've kissed her ugly sister
and loved her more.

Lay me down,
        lay me down
among the bodies of the living and the dead.
Even when the bed is dirty and cheap
        and the air conditioner
        hums "Amazing Grace"
                loudly,
                        over and over again.

Lay me down,
    lay me down
in the bed of history
so I can sleep with
the secrets of love lost,
    of love never found,
        of love that died, or was ruined.

I want to turn on the lights
and watch the cockroaches run for cover.

Let me sleep with construction workers and hookers,
once-rich stockbrokers on the fly from the law,
young women who left home for a new future,
    and destitute immigrants from Bombay.
    I am home everywhere,
especially when I am broke and travelling cheap—
because that is when I am most rich,
sleeping in the dust of my community.

    Lay me down, lay me down
    among the thousand bodies in the bed.
        I am ready
    to sleep in the arms of the world.

ONCE AGAIN, THE YELLOW SLATE MOUNTAIN
for Patrick Lane

When was the first time we travelled together?
Thirty years ago—and here we are on the road again,
back to the mountains, collecting slate for our gardens;
though these can hardly be called mountains,
shadowed by the glaciers of the Coast Range.
Call them hills, hummocks, rises, ridges, earth forced
into stone. How many friends have died since that first day
when we walked into the wilderness, adjusting our packs—
you with your rifle, me with my fish hooks?
A day that began years of arguments over dinners
and whiskies and women and wild rivers that
neither of us will see again in our lifetimes.
How many of our friends are gone now?
One walked into water. One spider-webbed his brains
with heroin and cocaine and an odd sense of adventure,
and another had her brains scrambled by her husband.
Several boiled in their own fiery alcoholic blood.
Cancer chased most of the rest. But some were unique,
you remember them, the ones who surprised us,
discovering spectacular ways to die in foreign zones.
Every year we return to this cliff-face, collecting slate
released by the freeze-and-thaw of mild winters—
gathering the prizes offered by natural erosion,
pathing each of our gardens like the countless other
gardeners who know this secret home of generous stone.
We're a joke now, growing old, staggering around
under the big slabs, just avoiding squashed fingers.
Why have we survived so long while the others died?
The doctors said I would go first, and here I am, stumbling

down the rutted road with my share of the mountain.
If we keep surviving like this, our arms full of rocks,
two aging men, laughing, going blind, limp, and weak,
we might yet end up taller than our yellow slate mountain.

GLACIAL MEMORIES

The orange tent on a snow ridge. I return often
to those years away from the city. The tumult—
it sends me there—the jarring hum of shopping malls,
the shouts and clangs, the unceasing electricity.

It was a moony night above the black basalt cliff, the river
of the glacier below sending its fingers into the horizon.
Behind me another glacier unrolled over the mountain.
There wasn't a tree in sight, and the cold soaked
into my bones until I became still, and the wind died
and the air filled with such unutterable calm
that I began to grow scared, paralyzed,
listening to the silent noise of the world.

III

WEIRD WEATHER

On the seventeenth day of snow,
    it snowed again.
The goose, at ten below,
made its break from beneath the porch
and floundered into the blizzard.
Later, when I shone the flashlight
on the humped mound of the snow-cave
    the concealed bird had created,
its head rose like a brontosaurus from a swamp.
    Lizards rising out of lizards.
    The extinction of species.
    Jurassic weather.

After the snow came the wind,
    came the sun, came the hail,
    came the deadly rain that stole
the road and smuggled it across the border
all the way down to a flooded Texas town.
    Crazy weather.
    My neighbours
speak in hushed tones of the next Ice Age,
islands that drown and are never seen again.
The crops die. The poisoners keep spraying.
We cultivate new tortures for the ozone.
    Chemical weather.
    Darkness weather.
    Weather like a prophecy.
I've seen it before, and I'm going to see it again—
the delights of erotic seasons when I was young,
the last strange wind that arrives for the old—
sunshine rainbows, and the scariness of snow fog
lying low on the ground, like the dragon's breath.

THE WOLF LOOKED UP

Was it only last night we chased
the aurora borealis, that array
of green and purple crackling
curtains in the surrealist film
optimistically called life on earth?
We thought we could catch
something, driving crazy and laughing
in an open jeep on those Yukon snow roads,
crashing through shadowy forests
        as we followed
the sky dreaming its colours.

Then, this morning, I stumbled upon her,
down by the breaking river, silver grey,
and staring at her reflection in the water.
The wolf looked up at me, and I knew
what I had been missing, what I had
thought I could find hunting rainbows,
while drunk, on snow-clogged roads so near
to the home of the wolf—I was searching
for perfect attention, when this
        is what it is.

ADVICE FOR A CHILD

Sit down and die, child,
only for a moment, only for me.
Listen to your heart slow, the breath
soften to quiet—torpid, ominous—die, child.
Or don't die, not now, but think about dying
tomorrow, perhaps this afternoon. You are
going to die when the sun cracks on the ridge.
Now look at that luminescent azalea, how
gorgeous it has become in the morning.
If you live until tomorrow, attend
to the dawn call of wild birds waking—
the excitement in their voices, a day
like a universe ahead. Listen to barking dogs.
Glance at the gaudy feathers of cardinals or jays,
their silkiness, the lustrous fur of a rabbit,
all the variations of green in a rain forest.
Walk barefoot in moss, or over rough rocks,
let the old story of sand ooze between your toes.
Decide you have leprosy, cerebral palsy, cancer,
and weep; then dream you were born legless,
or were raped at the river's edge, or had your ears
cut off for blood diamonds. Examine the wing
of the dragonfly, and mighty constellations
in elegant darkness on a mesa. Eat a fine soup,
eat dirt, eat nothing, watch your belly grow fat
with worms and malnutrition. Consider the many
thousand ways that you could be flung
into a shallow grave and still manage to see
one last glimpse of sky, immaculate, blue, forever.
Now live, child, live
inside the heart of each insane second that arrives.

GHAZAL WITH ITS THROAT CUT

If I give everything away
it's because I want to take everything.
John Thompson

No, the dead take it all.
(I have been waiting so long.)

Killing meat birds—each of us
has a different approach.

Windmills snapping the neck.
Hatchets. An icepick poking the brain.

I hesitated in the yard all morning.
Afraid of the house, the need

to carry these bloody hands inside.
45 dead chickens, plucked.

They were white once, like your night gown
when I lifted it last night.

Why is there no release? Why am I crying?
All those dead chickens? I don't think so.

Post coitum tristesse? Their approach to oblivion?
The fight, the cry, the kick?

The lean of a feathered head
against my shoulder, inert with sadness.

When I look in the cabinet
there are too many rifles—which one for me?

The tiny .22 hole in my temple? The shotgun blowout?
The lever-action Browning, a gift from a friend?

Then we go to school and we learn
to hold our head so no one can notice

we are already dead, bleeding from the throat.
There, the escaped one, stumbles in a green field.

I don't remember much any more.
And I don't know what I knew back then.

But I know the birds, the way
they perish with great tenderness.

WHITE RIDERS (INVISIBILITY)

Somewhere nearby it is forty below
and I've just awoken in this hotel room
in Whitehorse where the phone call
said my father was going to die,
that the cancer had him too,
and my dried-out eyes were burning,
and my pillow was damp with sweat,
and I was paralyzed on my bed,
startled by the hooves of fleeing horses,
and I began to think of invisibility
while listening to the sighs of the hotel;
all around me, the silence and the noise
of the night in this hive of human confusion—
and the woman in the thumping room above
is a squealer, a whooper, vocal and interesting,
and I remember two white horses running away,
and their riders had the same face, only years apart,
and I want to think I am with him,
that we will travel together again,
but she bucks and moans at each push
on the bed clattering directly overhead,
and I start to imagine how she is fucking,
and her voice betrays every thrust,
the quality of utterances giving clues
to depth and shifts of body weight and emotion,
and it's a long session, and I wish I knew her,
yet innocently, because she sounds original
and I've become sad and lost anyway,
but there are two riders wearing white slickers
in the dream I have suddenly failed,
and they have their hooded backs to me,

and the horses are on some snowy road,
and I thought I was only returning
from a desolate Watson Lake and Teslin
where the best pool players are the women
and the men drive their snowmobiles in fast circles,
and I think I spoke about poetry to someone,
and didn't know Father had been told he was a dead man,
and then I was driving the divide from Watson
in a blizzard punched apart suddenly by the geometry
of huge trucks that roared out of nowhere and blinded me—
or perhaps returned tonight as big, white, mist-snorting mares
with slickered riders, bursting from the sky and receding
on a long road between miles of storm-struck trees,
fading and fading and fading into the snow.

COMING HOME FROM DAWSON

Come to the edge. He said.
They said. We are afraid.
Come to the edge. He said.
They came.
He pushed them ... and they flew.
    Guillame Apollinaire,
    translator unknown,
    (from a real estate calender)

I was standing on the banks of the Yukon River
watching the ice break up and roll towards
the oblivion of the Bering Sea 1000 miles away.
Sharon and I were thinking about you all the time.
The phone call arrived near midnight,
and I knew we had to run. We slept restlessly.
I awoke at 4 a.m. By 5:47 we were on the road,
our departure timed to catch the opening
of the gas station in Carmacks, so we could
complete the dash to Whitehorse from Dawson.
    I'm coming home.
    I'm coming home, Dad.
    I'm coming home.
We passed four moose. You would have loved that.
You would have shouted, and called for your gun;
then announced with a wink: "Catch you next time."
    There were miles of road,
        hour after hour of driving past
        dead squirrels who'd insisted
        on suicide games with fast cars,
and hundreds of rabbits leaping for cover.
You would have laughed at the rabbits:

"Don't be afraid—we've already passed you."
And then a wolverine scurried in a circle on the road
like a low-flying rug possessed by demons.
You would have loved that, especially.

   I'm coming home.
   I'm coming home, Dad.
   I'm coming home.

This is all so much sentiment. I am full of it.
And I won't deny it. I will cry for days.
Already, my mother and my brothers and your brother
are taking their lonely places beside your bed,
but I am gone, as usual, far gone, yet driving hard for home.
They will listen to your breath, gaining hope with each one,
and terror as the gasps grow slower and further apart.

   I'm coming home.
   I'm coming home, Dad.
   I'm coming home.

This is not what I am supposed to write in a poem.
It is slush and embarrassing. I need a dignified voice
and passionless phrasing to speak of death in this age.
Well, fuck the voice. And the phrasing too.

   I'm coming home.
   I'm coming home, Dad.
   I'm coming home.

This poem is all wrong. It is a bad poem.
But I am still on the road, driving
through fire-burnt hills and mountain passes,
beyond skinny bears and dreams of love.
I will never see you alive again.
When I reach Whitehorse I will fill the corridors
of the hotel with one long howl
when I am told it is too late,
too late for life-and-death watches.

I will weep into glasses of whisky
in the tacky lounge at the Whitehorse airport
where someone will steal my credit card,
while all the young kids first adventuring
into the Yukon turn away and pretend
that me and this bad poem don't exist.
    I'm coming home.
    I'm coming home, Dad.
    I'm coming home.
I'm coming home with bad poems,
a ripped stomach, and miles of tears.
Miles and miles and miles of crying.

I arrived at a barren room
in a sterile hospital, the last place
where you ever wanted to die, but you
were guarded by two lively crows
standing sentry on the rail beyond the window.
On the wall hung a real estate calendar
where brightly clothed men and women
parachuted under words of hope.
Everyone who saw my weeping eyes
was kind, and they left me alone with you
and this terrible poem I had to write.
And for the first time in my life
    I kissed you on the lips,
but you were already dead and cold.

BE A MAN

Cleaning out the barn, the junk
of a working life, tools and gears,
and the glue clamps I never did use,
    the accumulations of a world
      made pointless by the new electronics.
Wiring, plumbing, horse gear, sheep hoof trimmers—
a life almost too far-fetched—grinders, and old motors
retained from my very first home, just in case....
Then, suddenly, boxes of alien things.
It takes me a few minutes to realize
they belonged to my dead father,
that by the usual osmosis of a family
they found their way into my barn.
I start to clear out the fishing tackle;
that's when the mask of efficiency begins to shred.
I count the years of his life by the lures in my hand:
the Black Mepps, the Crocodiles, the Tommy Jacks—
those decoys first cast against the rivers of his youth.
Then the Willow Spoons, the trolling lines for the big
Kamloops and Lake trout, sometimes the Brook,
stalked by a broad young man—his pretty wife
waiting dutifully on the shore amid a squall of kids—
the photograph almost a joke now, but so real then.
Later, there were the glory days of the saltchuck,
when he met the Coho and the big Spring salmon,
trolling off Rebecca or Kye Bay or Pourier Pass,
and discovered the complications of Mother too,
    as they became perfect companions,
finishing each other's sentences and baiting each other's hooks
    during those years when the oceans
      were a witch's brew of magnificent life.

And finally, they encountered the refinements
    of shore-casting together,
the deep lines and heavy steel gear
stashed in the basement when they both grew
too crippled to climb into the awkward boats.
    This is where I began weeping,
    because I have become once again
    the child he always hated in me.

THE BLUE DOE

I rest my hand on your radiant cloak.
The small hole
   in your chest
      is wet and stained with scarlet.
At my touch you give birth to your death,
give birth to the enormous silence of your eyes.

You are not watching me
while I sit beside your beauty.
   Do you know
   I am going to eat you?
My eyes are failing and I shot you badly.
   I could shoot you again,
   but you are already dying
and I haven't the heart to interfere
with your passage into the realm
   where all the dead deer go
when broken hooves
   or cougars
      or drought takes them,
even less gracefully than I have taken you.

I never loved the stupid, mindless thrill of the gun.
   Still, I know its lure,
a gift from hell sucking the heart out of some hunters.

Like D.H. Lawrence,
   I haven't seen an animal pity itself,
though I have seen them whimper with fear.
   So it is me who is weeping,

splashing my stupid tears
    on your immaculate hide,
and the grace of your death is a birth beside me.
    For a moment, I wonder
if we have been hunting each other for centuries,
    locked into the perpetual circle
        of birth and death.

    What wildness will come of this?
There will be feasts and laughter for my winter.
    Is that all you were born to feed?

Your luminous eyes look beyond my old, crippled body
    towards the hills
that are already part of your great forgetting and this birth,
    the remainder of the herd
        clicking over the rocks.

It was your colour that killed you,
    the slate blue-grey
signifying sterility and the nourishing fat
    destined to never feed a fawn.

Every hunter seeks the blue doe,
    the legend of her good meat.
That's why I chose you,
    not because you were like me,
one of a kind, fallow, useless to the future of the herd;
    and why we are here, together,
on a rocky bluff beside the arbutus pool
casting our tiny reflections back at us
    as we perform
this sad, private dance near the end of our lives.

EVENING MOVES OF A WOMAN AT FIFTY

So the moon knocked on her window,
knocked until she awoke, swimming in silver
and ghosts, while the bamboo outside
whispered the stories of the night.

Downstairs, she drank a glass of water.
The moonlight flooded the sun room,
pouring over the kitchen sink, fragrant
with its news of the green world.

Then among the shadows she found herself,
    found herself alive again
among the silvered leaves and six white flowers:
the six white flowers of the night-bloomer, larger than
dinner plates or a human skull, cactus-petalled,
streaming with scent, drowsy recollections, desire.
    And she travelled to Egypt.
    And she travelled to the Orient.
Frankincense. Myrrh. Sandalwood. Roses. Camphor.
The enormous aroma flowed over her; she was
    drinking it, the fragrance washing
    the folds of her naked body
written on by the luck of the years, elegantly stained
with work and children and flooding memory.

When she slipped back under the sheet beside him
she reached out, resting her hand on his flank—
stroking the same thigh she'd stroked for decades,
her own skin glowing, perfumed, freshly washed.

SENTIMENTALITY, OR MIDDLE-AGED DESIRE

When I am dead, burn me,
all the flesh and bones.
Use the fat of my fingers for candles;
they will light the way
through a few miles of dark.

O these fingers,
what they have touched—your body,
first of all, and often—alright, maybe not first
but they enjoyed undressing you
on the beach near Panama,
and behind the mangrove-styled alders
at Rennel Sound in the Charlottes,
in sad hotel rooms, wherever
love erupted among shadows.
I want it, still.
But yes, there were others.
I've been undressed by a few women also,
trembling, my little heart banging.
This was before my body collapsed,
but hey, there's no regret, just laughter,
gratitude for sunshine,
the night that follows,
and the dreams etched into my bones—
those haunted white birds of pain in the morning.

Everything is reach, desire,
even those languid stretches
before the bursts of energy
that suck our breath away,

only to blow it back into the lungs again,
just to remind us something has
portioned each person's years under the sun.
Our minds race towards experience.
     Especially those sugary dawns
     of orange and hasty clouds,
like the one where I was breathless for a moment
when I realized there was no meaning,
only the whirlpool, the quickening,
     the desire for meaning.
Or was that just desire itself,
     once again,
     brutal desire.

     So give it to me.
     I want it all. Everything.
Give me rocks when the tide retreats,
barnacles, and oolichans trapped in shallows
gasping for that ancient drink of salty life.
My old prostituted, junkie friends, what happened to them?
And the goofy, pileated woodpecker outside my window,
     knocking its head against a tree trunk—
     so loud that every morning
     I want to shoot it,
and then be haunted forever by the memory
     of having shot it.

     Give me everything.
I confess. I murdered exotic birds. I squirmed on top
of women I didn't love. I lied to my friends, the same way
they lied to me, elegantly, with the grace of a bird on a wire,
     a human pig in its pen.

I confess.
My head is on fire
with memory and desire.
They made me learn to love watching atomic explosions.
    They sing like the eye of a snake
lifting a lazy head and flicking its sexy tongue.
        Give it to me.
        Give me life.
        I want it.

My dad winking at me after he snapped his wooden leg.
    O Dad. O Dad. Where are you now?
Where's the frozen river resembling pearls cracked on rocks,
and the beautiful Labrador dog who sprang over the cliff,
    catching air?
Let's not forget the headless chicken haunting my childhood;
or the spastic mouse sneaking up behind the dumb cat,
    the way it ignited our laughter.
The spidery patina of frost on the brackens of autumn
that was imprinted behind the eye of childhood.
The Irish lad, Paddy, son of religious fanatics—
    a brittle boy dangling his snapped arm
    after falling from the tree.
And that little blonde girl whose hair rivered gold—
her secret life hidden behind acne and waxy, purple lips.

    Clean, cool sheets. The song of a cicada.
Water from a stream uncontaminated by misery.
Algae in a pond. Toe-biters and stick bugs, even leeches.
A few puffy clouds drifting in an impossible sky.
I want it all complicated, and I want it all simple.
Meditation in a dark room. Silence.
    The cornucopia of austerity.

Yes, and I want my baroque cake, too,
decorated with green icing and fake roses.

I've decided I want to die
the way I have lived.
Give me everything.
Then send me out to the edge.

No, I won't cling to the last breath,
dragging my fingernails across the dirt.
I'm going to fold up my tent
and go away ... away ... away....

The sound of that word—away—
like a far-off bird,
distant, looking for sleep
as the sun smacks the horizon
and then forgets itself
in the lazy moments before darkness.

When I consider my ruined knees and broken promises,
my years of shining and my debt load,
my old dog dying of some tumours and age,
the way that horned moon above the mountain
reflects a different turquoise sky every sunfall,
I can't help but remember being
crippled and celebrated and tortured and loved.
And I need to give thanks—give thanks again—
then give some more thanks for my life on earth,
because time is unwinding, and I'm going to die soon.

I want all of it.

ORGANIC GENETIC CONDITION

Every time I look at my mutant body
I see the art of nature written sideways.
But when the dawn's crimson light hits me,
alone, once again facing the world's wall
and I want to put the gun to my head,
I inhale the air and wonder at the magic,
the crazy life that dances its disease
out of the nervous beauty of wounds.
There are secrets everywhere. Millions of them.
They are confusions like gold dust in the hand,
 glittering and then gone
 as all becomes memory,
which is just a variety of laughter.

Yet there was another time, another century,
when the child I was, born weird, would have been
exposed to the glorious rain on a mountain.
 It would have been known then
as sorrow, and the way we should live, natural.

WHEN I LIE WITH THE DYING LAMB

When I lie with the dying lamb
in the manger, I desire so little,
because life is already
more than I can take,
nestled in the hay, listening
to the gasps of tiny breath—the hiss
of the propane lantern hanging overhead.
The mother is dead in the corner,
and soon death will follow death
as it has done for the millenniums
since this unholy mess invented itself
in a chemical fog that should
make any thinking creature bitter.

How our blood surges for the newborn,
the gorgeous miracle and enigma—
though we will slaughter this lamb
for meat in four months if it survives,
which it won't. Death is seconds away.
I look into its eyes, seeking the mystery,
but they are already filled with the secrets
        of the other side, the place
        where we can't go, until we go.
And I lie still in the hay, holding the black hoof
of a dead lamb—feeling left behind once again,
        uninstructed.

FIREWEED
for Peter, in his house

After the fire comes the flower.
    In the slashy hills,
    in the creek bottoms
where the loggers have walked,
    I could see their mauve river
riding the burnt hills into the Yukon autumn.
Fireweed, that first flower, rages across
the old, bald mountain and the stony mountain,
fighting for life with the poplars and willows
as they fade to yellow and then auburn.
Fireweed erupts across the continent—
feeds shadows, dampness, alders,
aspen, pines, firs, squirrels
rats, mice, crows, hawks.
    Here they come,
    the treasures of the forest,
wolverines, Siberian wolves, blue foxes,
more rats, hunters, housewives, children,
tanners, sowers and reapers, blacksmiths.
    They just keep on coming—the shacks,
the many avenues, the dreaming future.
    Rebuilding and rebirthing.
Pass me the second one, she said, *and I will*
give her the other breast to suckle.
Hammers, arrowheads, plows, hairpins.
The world goes multitudinous with confusion:
towns, cities, megacities, street kids.
The rats grow fatter, the wheat grows thicker,
gorgeous life, wealth, panties dropped, dishware,
strip malls, home entertainment units.

It gets crazier:
riots, wars, the last pigeon circling a ringed moon,
    and fire again—
melting the ground, melting faces,
and then, and then, the laughter
the little shrieks of love, the fireweed
    teaching me
I need to be burned to be reborn.

MOON OF NEW LAMBS

Every season has its strength, each moon
flowing into the river of stars overhead.
I live with what arrives at the door,
in the saffron of the dawn, or the twilight
of my legs giving out, learning the natural—
holding life in my hands when it dies, giving
earth to friends that I let go. The world
is not real and I fit it like a badly made glove.
But I get up in the morning and work; I work
forever until the ceasing day makes me a liar, and I quit—
passing all that work to the hands of the night
where the secret iridescent leaves continue bursting
and the epileptic lamb shuts down its electric breath.
But the fields are never ending ... never ... never ...
ending pastures of meadow maggots, or sheep
as I sometimes call them, breeding endlessly,
breeding bitterly, anxiously, joyously, cravenly—
       creation after creation,
wonder after wonder—out of the gore leaps
       more life.

NIGHT DIRECTIONS FOR THE LOST

Turn left when you pass the frog
barking under the pumphouse
and follow alongside the brown bats
dipping low above the pond.
Since all is near-invisible you can name everything.
We will let you give words to the dark.
Call back your memories,
the kasbah in Casablanca,
the fragrant alleys behind Main Street
where the hookers shot dreams into their arms.
The road that led to where it ended.
Call this a thistleseed, call that a fence.
Call it all the wheel of the world.
Call it the whispering pasture under your feet.
And that noise like a marble falling down stairs,
call it the owl celebrating the mouse it swallowed,
    call your heart alive and pounding,
call yourself a human being who sings in the shadows.
Name the animals, name the plants, name yourself,
and keep on going until you can call it paradise.

ALSO BY BRIAN BRETT

Fossil Ground at Phantom Creek
Smoke Without Exit
Evolution in Every Direction
The Fungus Garden
Tanganyika
Poems: New and Selected
Allegories of Love and Disaster
The Colour of Bones in a Stream
Coyote, A Mystery

CD
Night Directions for the Lost